PEACEMAKING:
A CHRISTIAN VOCATION

A resource for the churches produced by a joint working group of the
United Reformed Church and Methodist Church.

Centre for
Faith and Spirituality
Loughborough Universi⁺

The
United
Reformed
Church

86 Tavistock Place
London WC1H 9RT

The **Methodist** Church

25 Marylebone Road
London NW1 5JR

ISBN 1-85852-323-0   EAN 978-1-85852-323-1

Blessed are the peacemakers,
for they will be called the children of God.
(Matthew 5:9)

PREFACE

In the post cold war era, the challenge of reducing tension and securing peace seems as elusive as ever. Global power dynamics have been transformed by the influence of a major superpower and the rapid extension of market forces. Meanwhile, military technology has developed substantially and defence forces are being reconfigured to tackle new threats. In 2003, public debate about the proposed intervention in Iraq was hampered by the confidentiality of intelligence information and the strong rhetoric that now comes with the 'war on terror'. Given these challenges what contribution should the Church make to public discourse on peace and security?

This report fulfils a desire on the part of both the United Reformed Church and Methodist Church to re-examine the ethics of war in the current context. The United Reformed Church General Assembly asked its Church and Society Committee to explore and prepare a report on the ethics of warfare for the twenty first century and to work ecumenically and internationally in this task. In 2004, the Methodist Council approved a joint collaboration with the United Reformed Church in this endeavour. Following consultation, a working group was formed drawing together diverse views from both the Methodist Church and United Reformed Church. The first meeting of the working group was held in May 2005 where the wide-ranging and general brief was narrowed to limit the scope to that which could reasonably be satisfied in one succinct report. For example we have avoided any extensive analysis on the nature of terrorism but refer in a bibliography to resources that can inform further.

The intention is to provide a study that a) stimulates reflection within and beyond our churches, b) provides an ethical analysis to help to support the judgement of the church and church leaders in complex and uncertain situations where British military intervention is proposed. Any such exercise is by nature incomplete and we welcome criticism and development of the arguments expounded in this report.

The working group comprised people with diverse backgrounds including seasoned peace activists, a military chaplain, a minister who formerly served on nuclear submarines and academic theologians with relevant specialities. A wider range of written material was reviewed and consultations held with key facilitators. We are grateful to Dr Charles Reed, Dr Judith May Parker and General Sir Hugh Beach, each of whom met with the group and provided insightful and candid input in specific areas of our study.

A total of four meetings were held between May and November 2005 with an intensive programme of work in between. A most pleasing aspect of the exercise has been the way in which the members have overcome difference within the group despite passionately held views. All members have contributed to the preparation of this report. We are grateful to their diligent work and contribution under considerable pressure of time and the rigours of their other responsibilities. In particular we are indebted to Dr David Clough who has pulled together the material into a unified whole and worked with the group to refine the final text. We are grateful too for twelve people who undertook to read a draft of the report and offer comments.

We offer this material for study by all who seek to reflect and offer comment on some of the complex issues of war, justice and peace today.

STEVE HUCKLESBY
Methodist Church
Secretary for International Affairs

PHILIP WOODS
United Reformed Church
Secretary for International Relations

MEMBERSHIP OF THE WORKING GROUP

Revd Dr Peter Bishop (Co-convenor)

Revd John Johansen-Berg (Co-convenor)

Revd Hazel Barkham

Dr David Clough

Revd Paul Jupp

Revd Mike Parker

Revd Jennifer Potter

Dr Esther D. Reed

Steve Hucklesby (Working Group Secretary)

Revd Philip Woods (Working Group Secretary)

SUMMARY

In 2003 the proposed war in Iraq caused many who had never protested before to take to the streets. However popular engagement in the cause of peace was much too late. For decades Western self-interest had resulted in damaging and confused policies towards Iraq and the scene was now set for a bloody conflict. Many within our churches and beyond are asking searching questions concerning the capacity of governments and the international system to promote peace and maintain order. The study aims to help us on the journey towards a common understanding of ethical principles informed by our Christian tradition.

Having outlined the task ahead, the second chapter *Learning from the Past*, reviews Christian tradition on the subject. There are several passages in the Old Testament apparently advocating total war or massacre. We must understand the context of these texts and recognize that they must not be interpreted as sanctioning such acts in the present.

The New Testament also raises difficult questions. We engage with these but ultimately conclude that God's will for peace is unequivocal. The Bible canon, taken as a whole, provides a profound witness to the value of life and peace. This survey of biblical texts is complemented by an overview of the development of different attitudes to warfare in Christian history, from early pacifism to the Just War and on to the total wars of the twentieth century and the new threat of terrorism.

In addressing questions of peace and war, it is crucial for Christians to recall with profound regret the way that the medieval church endorsed the use of wars fought for the sake of religion in the crusades. Nevertheless we explore here how our rich Christian heritage and perspectives of other faiths might help us interpret anew the call to be peacemakers today. The call to become peacemakers is the theme for the next chapter, *Building for Peace*.

Jesus' call to be peacemakers is directed to everyone but it is neither simple to discern nor easy to follow. This call is as relevant to our personal and professional relationships as it is in the national or international setting. The Church carries a responsibility to help each member to work out their calling to be Christ's witness in the world yet it too often retreats within comfort zones of familiar debates.

In the years ahead our notions of security will be based less on the presence of national security forces to protect us from threats outside or within and increasingly on our success in tackling global threats such as climate change. A clearer discernment of God's calling to be peacemakers might lead us to more concerted political action.

The instinct to retaliate or assert control over conflict is all too common. Chapter 4 seeks to illuminate some *Non-violent Strategies for Dealing with Conflict.*

Violence finds many manifestations in the home, school or workplace, in video games and in real life. The study turns to the experiences of Gandhi, Martin Luther King as well as social and political movements in Eastern Europe to understand how power by force has been challenged. To achieve progress in non-violence training is essential and adequate resources need to be allocated. Some examples of training by NGOs are described.

Equally we can recount situations where warlords appear to be able to act with impunity. Chapter 5, *'On the Use of Force'* deals with the uncomfortable realities of conflict. In addressing the question of military force the study group took time to read and hear first hand the experiences of those caught up in conflict. Some accounts are retold here. Can Christians ever support the threat or use of military force and if so under what circumstances?

Sin and corruption are an inevitable part of our existence and our earthly authorities are necessarily charged with the application of law, the responsibility to protect using impartial judgement and the maintenance of order. The report contends that violence is always alien to God's reign but recognizes that temporal authority is, by nature, coercive rather than persuasive.

Right authority necessitates an element of objective judgement. It is argued that authority to pursue war cannot be reduced to an assertion of a nation's right to self-defence. The implications are explored in the context of the strengths and weaknesses of the UN system.

Having established some theological foundations the chapter offers some insights regarding genocide, terrorism, pre-emptive war, nuclear weapons and arms control. We note the significant peacemaking opportunity the UK currently has to decide against embarking on a costly successor to the Trident nuclear weapons system and call on the churches to argue against its replacement.

Consideration of appropriate responses to any specific conflict must be subordinated to the primary goal of peacemaking. The concluding chapter proposes some practical aspects to the *Christian Vocation of Peacemaking*. Four dimensions to peacemaking are explored, a) fostering just and peaceful relationships, b) being active in resolving conflicts c) supporting strategies for preventing violent conflict and d) engaging with political leaders about how and when violent force might be used.

Taking a stand against powerful interests in the name of peace is a risky business that has cost some peacemakers their lives. This aspect of mission is poorly understood and the individuals and organisations involved need our support.

Those holding pacifist and just war positions have more in common than is at first apparent. In this concluding section we identify a common agenda and lay this before our churches to stimulate reflection. This report is offered in the context of an ongoing dialogue but it is also presented as a call to action. The Church cannot claim to have a monopoly on truth and neither can our governments. Ultimately this report invites bold and effective leadership from the churches in the cause of peace.

1

PEACE:
SEEKING A COMMON UNDERSTANDING

1.1 In February 2003, many UK Christians travelled to London and Glasgow to protest against the planned invasion of Iraq, joining millions of many faiths and none in 800 cities worldwide to form the largest ever mass demonstration. Church leaders in the UK had consistently opposed going to war without the support of the United Nations, and opinion polls showed that the nation agreed. Those protesting were outraged at what was to be done in their name. In bringing their concern for peace before those in authority, the Christians who marched were acting in continuity with a long Christian tradition, going back at least as far as Bishop Ambrose of Milan, who in AD 390 called the Roman Emperor Theodosius I to account for the massacre of more than 7000 citizens of Thessalonica. Christians believe that peace is God's fundamental will for the created order and that they have a responsibility to witness to this truth to those in power.

1.2 While Christians have been unanimous in affirming peace as the will of God, they have not been univocal about whether war is a legitimate means to this peace. The earliest Christians understood Jesus' teaching as making the use of violence illegitimate for Christians,[1] but later generations of believers came to the understanding that a war fought for the right reason and in the right way could be a way of expressing the Christian responsibility to love the neighbour. Since the 4th century AD, the latter view that war could sometimes be justified has been the majority view among Christians, but there has always been a minority maintaining that the only way to be obedient to the teaching of Christ is to renounce violence altogether.

[1]For examples of this, see paragraph 2.5, below.

1.3   In this report, we acknowledge this divergence of view between the just war tradition and pacifism, which is represented both in the membership of the Methodist and United Reformed Churches in the United Kingdom, and in the members of this group. This report also argues, however, that just as both of these views share a common understanding of God's call to human beings to live in peace, so they also share a common agenda for active peacemaking. We believe that the churches must continue to struggle prayerfully with the Bible, the Christian tradition, and the current international context in order to understand whether going to war can be the will of God. But we also consider it crucial for all Christians, whatever their beliefs on this issue, to recognize their common vocation as peacemakers. This report therefore examines what is necessary to build for peace and what new questions are raised by the realities of warfare at the beginning of the twenty-first century, with the aim of assisting our churches and their members to discern how our calling to be peacemakers may be expressed in action. During our reflections, we have tried to be attentive to voices that are often ignored: civilians subjected to military attack and those serving in the armed forces.

1.4   The first part of the report sets our discussion of peace and violence in the context of the Bible and the history of the church through a brief survey. Obviously we cannot do justice to the entirety of Christian discussion of these questions: our aim is to outline the theological basis for the positions we take later in the report. We then turn to the question of what kind of practices are likely to reduce the number of occasions when nations resort to war, before turning to examine what are the new questions raised by modern warfare, and how the resulting challenges may be addressed. We highlight in particular the dire consequences of war for the environment and argue that the just war criterion of proportionality needs to be expanded to reckon seriously with this consideration. The conclusion to the report sets out key priorities for action by churches that we believe to belong to the vocation of peacemaking for Christians in the UK at this time.

2

LEARNING FROM THE PAST

2.1 From the beginnings of salvation history in the Garden of Eden, to its end in the New Jerusalem, the Bible witnesses to the profound value of life and peace. God is portrayed in Genesis 6 as causing the great flood because of human corruption and violence, and afterwards announces that a reckoning will be demanded of any one that takes human life, because humans bear the divine image (Genesis 9:5-6). The Bible looks forward to a time when there will be no more violence, notably in Isaiah's vision of God's holy mountain where no life of any kind will be destroyed (Isaiah 11:6–9) and in the Revelation of St. John of the new heaven and earth where God will wipe away all tears, and there will be no more death, crying, or pain (Revelation 21:4). Isaiah and Micah share the vision of a time when God will judge between nations, when they will beat swords into ploughshares and spears into pruning hooks and there will be no more war (Isaiah 2:4; Micah 4:3). Jesus teaches in the Sermon on the Mount that it will be the peacemakers that will be called the children of God (Matthew 5:9) and that his followers should turn the other cheek when struck, love their enemies, and pray for their persecutors (Matthew 5:39–45). This teaching is echoed in Paul's letter to the Romans (12:14–21) and the letter of James echoes Jesus' praise of peacemakers: 'a harvest of righteousness is sown in peace for those who make peace' (James 3:18). The Letter to the Hebrews calls Jesus 'king of peace' (7:2) and calls on church members to 'pursue peace with everyone' and 1 Thessalonians calls on the sanctification of the 'God of peace'. And in the epistles the work of Christ itself is described as making peace, most obviously in Colossians 1:20: 'through him God was pleased to reconcile to himself all things, whether on earth or in heaven, by making peace through the blood of his cross'.

2.2 Alongside this strong affirmation of the priority of peace in the Bible, we must acknowledge passages that are more troubling. For Jews and Christians, the most disturbing texts relating to warfare in the Bible are the parts of the law documenting how Israel is to fight, and the stories of their slaughter of neighbouring tribes at the command of God. Deuteronomy 20 sets out the standards of conduct expected. For distant nations, Israel is to offer peace. If the offer is accepted, the population is subjected to forced labour; if it is not accepted, after the battle all the males are to be killed and the women and children taken as spoils of war (Deuteronomy 20:10–15). For nations living within the land God has given Israel, an even harsher standard applies: 'you must not let anything that breathes remain alive' (Deuteronomy 20:16). Next to these shocking texts, we must place the narrative of 1 Samuel 15, where God commands Saul to slaughter the Amalekites 'both man and woman, child and infant, ox and sheep, camel and donkey' (1 Samuel 15:3). Saul spares the king and the best of the animals, and as a result loses favour with God. There is no escaping these difficult texts, all the more disturbing given our over-familiarity with genocidal crimes in the last century, in Nazi Germany, Rwanda, and elsewhere.

2.3 How are we to deal with these texts? First, we should note that the massacres commanded and narrated in the Old Testament must be seen in the context of Israel's concern about purity as a key component of what it meant to be holy before God. The concern that the Israelites should not fall into the ways of the peoples already living in the land they occupy is of a piece with the concern not to wear clothes of two cloths, and the elaborate rituals to avoid uncleanliness. We should therefore bear in mind that the legal prescriptions in Deuteronomy, and even the subsequent narratives of massacres after battle, may be religiously idealized views of what it meant for Israel to be holy, rather than an accurate guide to what actually took place. Secondly, we should recognize that the crucial emphasis is on God fighting for Israel, and the kings who seek to build up large armies are criticized for not putting their trust in God (e.g. Isaiah 30:15-16): these texts are by no means an uncritical endorsement of militarism. Finally, we must read these texts in the context of the rest of the biblical canon, in which God's will for peace is unequivocal, and our saviour Jesus Christ is recognized as the Prince of Peace (Isaiah 9:6). For all these reasons, texts recounting the wars fought by Israel and instruction for how they are to be conducted are no basis for justifying the use of violence in the present. Obviously any use of them to support crusades, unlimited war or genocide in the present would be illegitimate to the point of obscenity.

2.4   There are also a few New Testament texts that sit oddly with the otherwise consistent emphasis on peace. According to Luke, John the Baptist did not tell soldiers to leave the army (Luke 3:14), and Luke also has Jesus telling the disciples at the Last Supper they should buy swords if they do not have them (Luke 22:36-38). Jesus teaches that he comes to bring not peace, but a sword (Matthew 10:34). In his letter to the Romans, Paul affirms the right of government to wield the sword (Romans 13:1–5). Alongside this, the astonishingly violent imagery of war in the Book of Revelation must give us pause, where John recounts his vision of the defeat and destruction of swathes of God's enemies. None of these passages, however, should lead us to set aside the strong witness of the New Testament against the use of violence. The astonishing feature of the story of John the Baptist is that Roman soldiers as foreign occupying forces paid any attention to him at all, and that John did not denounce their profession does not mean he approved it. At the Last Supper, Jesus is warning the disciples of the opposition they will face in the next phase of their ministry, and any more literal interpretation is ruled out by Jesus' lack of patience with the attempted violent resistance of the disciples later that evening when a crowd came to arrest him (Luke 22:49-51). Jesus' reference to coming to bring a sword is obviously metaphorical, and his observation that his message may provoke conflict within families is preparing his followers for hard times ahead, rather than contradicting the consistent testimony that God's desire is for peace. Similarly, the recognition in Romans 13 that the state is given the authority to bear the sword by God is not an exception to God's will for peace, but the recognition that the state may have to use force to maintain temporal peace. (As we note below, this text became important for later Christians who had to consider whether Christians should assist the state in this task.) Finally, the message of Revelation is that the church should endure and trust in God's power to redeem them, so cannot be cited in support of a human bearing of arms.

2.5 While the Bible is clear that God's will is for peace, we have already recognized that Christians have come to different views about how this should be achieved. The first Christians interpreted the teaching of Jesus as prohibiting the use of any kind of violence. Justin Martyr (c.110–165) claims the peacefulness of Christianity fulfils Isaiah's prophecy of swords being beaten into ploughshares: 'we who formerly used to murder one another do not only now refrain from making war upon our enemies, but also…willingly die confessing Christ'.[2] At the end of the second century, Clement of Alexandria (c.150–c.215) similarly contrasts war and peace: 'It is not in war, but in peace, that we are trained. War needs great preparation, and luxury craves profusion; but peace and love, simple and quiet sisters, require no arms nor excessive preparation'. In another work he instructs the rich to gather 'an unarmed, an unwarlike, a bloodless, a passionless, a stainless host'. Tertullian (c.160 – 225) addresses the issue of military service forthrightly: 'But how will a Christian man war, nay, how will he serve even in peace, without a sword, which the Lord has taken away?' 'Shall it be held lawful to make an occupation of the sword, when the Lord proclaims that he who uses the sword shall perish by the sword? And shall the son of peace take part in the battle when it does not become him even to sue at law?' And Origen (c.185–c.254) is similarly uncompromising, explaining Christians 'no longer take up 'sword against nation', nor do we 'learn war any more', having become children of peace, for the sake of Jesus, who is our leader'.

---

[2] Justin Martyr, *First Apology*, ch. 39, *The Ante-Nicene Fathers*, A. Cleveland Coxe, James Donaldson and Alexander Roberts, eds (Edinburgh: T & T Clark, 1997), vol. 1, 175–6.

2.6 Roman soldiers were required to take part in military religious rites, and some have suggested that objection to idolatry, rather than objections to killing, was the motive for prohibiting military service. Others have pointed to examples where Christians did serve in the military in the second and third centuries, notably those who fought for the 'Thundering Legion', whose prayers Tertullian and others cited as leading to miraculous rainfall that rescued a campaign in AD 173.[3] It is clear, however, that Christians objected to military service on the grounds that use of the sword was prohibited to them, as well as concern about participation in military cultic rites. While these objections were not uniformly successful in preventing Christians enlisting in the Roman army, they were the established view of the pre-Constantinian church, represented in church orders as late as the third century, as well as the writings of many Christian leaders.

[3] Tertullian, *Apology*, ch. 5 (*Ante Nicene Fathers*, vol. 3, 22). For other examples of Christian participation in the Roman army, see John Helgeland, Robert J. Daly, and J. Patout Burns, *Christians and the Military: The Early Experience* (London: SCM Press Ltd, 1987).

2.7   The breathtaking change in the social location of the church following the conversion of the
Emperor Constantine from sun worship to Christianity in AD 313 led to a major upheaval in
Christian thinking about war. Christians suddenly found themselves transformed from a
persecuted sect to a prominent position of influence within the empire, and had quickly to
come to terms with their new status. While Bishop Ambrose (c.339–397) challenged the
violence of Theodosius I, in the first generation of the newly Christian Roman Empire he
had no difficulty in recognizing the common interest in defending the empire against the
barbarians: 'Not eagles and birds must lead the army, but thy name and religion, O Jesus'.
Only clergy were exempt from the permission to participate in the military and former
soldiers together with civil magistrates and murderers were forbidden to enter holy orders.
By AD 416, however, the shift in Christian thinking made it possible for Theodosius II to
issue an edict specifying that only Christians could serve in the army. Following Ambrose,
Augustine (354–430) began to develop a framework for Christian judgement about when
war could be justified: the cause of war must be just, it must be declared by a legitimate
political authority, and the authority must be rightly motivated in doing so. Augustine's
thinking was systematized and expanded by a series of theologians, most notably Thomas
Aquinas (1225–1274), Francisco de Vitoria (c.1486–1546), Francisco Suarez (1548–1617)
and Hugo Grotius (1583–1645). This Just War tradition of thinking encompassed a series of
criteria for when it was right to go to war (known by the Latin term *jus ad bellum*),
together with principles for what conduct was acceptable during war (*jus in bello*). To the
jus ad bellum criteria were added those of last resort — stipulating that non-violent options
for resolving the conflict must have been exhausted — and proportionality — requiring that
the war looks likely to bring about more good than harm. The jus in bello criteria prohibit
the intentional targeting of non-combatants and require that actions within wars as well as
the wars themselves are proportionate to their ends. There has always been a witness to the
alternative of pacifism through monastic communities and churches such as the
Anabaptists, Mennonites, Hutterites, Society of Friends and the Brethren, and this tradition
also continues to be represented in other denominations, including the Methodist and
United Reformed Churches. For the last 1600 years, however, the evolving Just War
tradition has been the majority position of the Christian church.

2.8   In addressing questions of peace and war, it is crucial for Christians to recall with profound regret the way that the medieval church endorsed the use of wars fought for the sake of religion in the crusades. This was a disastrous episode in the history of the church, in which Christian warriors, encouraged by the church that they were doing God's will, were guilty of appalling violence against Muslims, and were encouraged to attack Jews in the Christian homelands. The crusades cast a long shadow, and the violence of groups such as Al Qaeda today looks back to past Christian violence as justification.

2.9   A brief comparison with some of the main ideas found in Judaism and Islam may help to shed light on what is shared and what is distinctive in the Abrahamic traditions. It is fitting that Christians approach Jewish and Islamic traditions in great humility, aware of, on the one hand, many centuries of Christian anti-Semitism, and on the other hand a history of colonialism that subjugated Islamic territories. We also need to acknowledge that members of all three Abrahamic faiths engage in constant efforts to understand and interpret their own scriptures within which are verses that, taken literally, appear to condone or even encourage violence. In Judaism, while there is no strong tradition of pacifism, Rabbinic interpretations of *Torah* emphasize the priority of peace over war, in keeping with which Maimonides said that: 'one may never wage war with anyone until one has first made an offer of peace'. Wars must be declared and legally endorsed, mass destruction is illicit, and the future vitality of the land is an important moral consideration.[4] The general view in Islam is that war is hateful, and paradise is the land of peace – dar al-Islam. War is justifiable only where necessary to prevent the triumph of evil. Three different Arabic words are used in connection with conflict. The primary meaning of *jihad* is not fighting, but struggling for the sake of the faith. By contrast *qittal* means killing; and *harb* refers to the land in which Islamic faith is formally upheld. In Islamic teaching there are rulings on the conduct and termination of wars, and on relations between Muslims and non-Muslims that are close to the Christian Just War doctrine.[5]

---

[4] For further information, see Albert B. Randall, *Theologies of War and Peace Among Jews, Christians and Muslims* (Lewiston N.Y: The Edwin Mellen Press, 1998).

[5] See Harfiyah Abdel Haleem et al, *The Cross and the Crescent. Muslim and Christian Approaches to War and Peace* (Basingstoke, Hampshire: Palgrave MacMillan, 1988).

2.10 Events in the twentieth century changed the context for thinking about peace and war dramatically. Even before the First World War, there were large protests by organized labour against sending workers to die in a war in which they had no stake. The mass killing of troops during the war gave rise to a widespread disillusion about warfare as a means of resolving conflicts and to a consequent growth in peace movements in Europe. Alongside this, there was widespread admiration for the non-violent action in the campaign led by Mahatma Gandhi against the British Empire in India. Gandhi's peaceful protests inspired many pacifists to believe that they did not have to sacrifice effectiveness in combating injustice when they rejected the use of violence. The issue of effectiveness provoked hard questions for the peace movement: should non-violent action be promoted as the most effective means to address particular kinds of conflicts, or was it a moral demand, irrespective of the consequences? The Second World War persuaded many that non-violence was not likely to be effective against all opponents, though non-violent action was politically important after the war in the shape of anti-nuclear protests in Europe and anti-Vietnam protests in the United States. The deliberate targeting of civilians in the bombing of German and Japanese cities clearly contravened just war principles, and the atomic bombs dropped by the US on Hiroshima and Nagasaki took this policy to a horrific new level. Many concluded after the war that in a nuclear age, just wars were no longer possible. Concern after the Second World War about the continuing threat of war between nation states led to the institutions of the United Nations and the European Union.

2.11 Already, the twenty-first century has provoked a great deal of new reflection and discussion about warfare. Many were hopeful entering a new millennium that nations could learn to find more peaceful ways of coexisting, but these aspirations were rudely dashed by the attacks on the World Trade Centre and the Pentagon on 11th September 2001, and the wars launched by the US in the aftermath in Afghanistan and Iraq. There is a perception that the world is a more dangerous place than it seemed at the end of the twentieth century, and the UK together with other nations has responded by introducing new legislation restricting civil liberties at home, and fighting a war in Iraq on the grounds of its supposed possession of nuclear, chemical and biological weapons. This is the new world context in which we must address the question of what it means to be peacemakers.

3

BUILDING FOR PEACE

3.1   Peacemaking is at the heart of the teaching of Jesus, not an optional extra. But is there a connection today between this truth and politics at the global level? What strategies for peacemaking and the prevention of war might the Church pursue? Hard thinking about the Church's unique contribution to national and international debates is required to answer such questions. So, we state the question as follows: Is there a connection between the eternal peace of God that belongs to the new creation, wrought for us by God through the death and resurrection of Jesus Christ, and human strategies for peacemaking in the face of wars and conflicts? Is there an inward and vital connection between peace with God through our Lord Jesus Christ (Romans 5:1) – which is the primary reality to which the Church points – and the peacebuilding that we need so desperately around the globe today?

3.2   The mystery that we have 'peace with God through our Lord Jesus Christ' because through him we have obtained access to grace (Romans 5:1-2) can, and must, be distinguished from human attempts at peacemaking. But 'to distinguish' is not the same as 'to divide', 'to separate' or 'to juxtapose'. As Dietrich Bonhoeffer wrote: 'There are not two competing realms standing side by side and battling over the borderline, as if this question of boundaries was always the decisive one.'6 Rather, the whole reality of the world is drawn to God in Christ and belongs ultimately to him (Ephesians 1:20-1; 1 Peter 3:22). The peace that Christ Jesus won over sin and death is the reason, and the ground upon which, we dare to speak of principalities, powers and 'rulers of the darkness of this world' (Ephesians 6:12).

---

6 Dietrich Bonhoeffer, *Ethics* Dietrich Bonhoeffer Works, Volume 6. From GE eds Ilse Tödt, et al., English ed Clifford J. Green, transl. Reinhard Krauss, et al. (Minneapolis: Fortress Press, 2005), p.58

3.3   Jesus' message was not bland (Matthew 6:1-6; 16-18; 23:27), his actions were often unpopular with both crowds and those in power (Luke 13:31, 15:1-2; John 7:20-32) and, when necessary, he took direct action (Mark 11:15-19; Luke 19:45-47). 'In all strands of the gospel tradition, Jesus is not a figure readily associated with peace in the sense of visible harmony. He provokes conflict and confrontation, and says truly enough that he brings not peace but a sword (Matthew 10:43), that he comes to kindle a fire on the earth (Luke 12:49). …. It would be a fatal reduction of the Gospel to say that Jesus' work is simply the revelation of universal brotherhood [sic].[7] Jesus was not a political zealot but called followers to a new way of living which sometimes deepened rather than healed existing wounds, subverted treasured harmonies of family and professional life, and intensified dilemmas. His peace is not as the world gives (John 14:27) and his reign is not of this world (John 18:36). In Christian belief, true justice is found in his reign.

---

[7] Rowan Williams, *The Truce of God: Peacemaking in Troubled Times* (Norwich: Canterbury Press, 1985 / 2005), pp. 67-68.

3.4 What, then, might it mean today to follow Christ, the Prince of Peace? Response to this call can take a wide range of forms: preaching of the gospel in services of worship and the discipline of prayer through which the Church does, and should, proclaim God's peace to the world; non-violent demonstration; long term campaigning to expose and overcome corruption; political lobbying for the removal of injustice and oppression wherever it occurs; regular donations to Non-Governmental Organisations working for reconciliation in war zones; engagement in local, global or international politics for peace; collaborating with other faith groups in peacemaking and conflict transformation initiatives; writing history books or newspaper articles to further critical analysis of the characteristics of lasting peace; and much more. Our working group comprised seasoned protestors at nuclear sites and military installations, alongside those working for the British Armed Forces, or recently retired. For the former, the Christian Campaign for Nuclear Disarmament, and similar organisations, are the most powerful means of faith-based opposition to nuclear and other weapons of mass destruction. For others, the role of the Church is best described as 'Critical Companion' of the state as the state predicts and provides for the defence needs of the country; the role of earthly governance in divine providence requires the Church to work with and pray for governments wherever they act for the common good.

3.5 One crucial focus in building for peace in the current context is attending to environmental issues that will otherwise become sources of conflict. Members of the churches need to remain alert and critical both with respect to our own practice and our assessment of what we humans are doing one to another, and not doing for one another, around the globe. We live in a globalised world where actions in one country have repercussions all around the earth. Competition for scarce resources such as oil, gas and water supplies has already been the cause of conflict between nations and is set to become an even greater source of conflict in the future unless action is taken to reduce and diversify resource use and to set up international bodies to broker agreements on more equitable utilisation. With changes brought about by global climate change, agricultural and marine resources may well also become a source of potential conflict. As a whole range of resources become scarcer and available in ever more inaccessible places, competition for access to them will become fiercer.

3.6   The question of global warming and climate change is in itself a highly charged issue between the countries of the developed world and of the developing, mainly southern, world. It is the 'global north' whose industrial activities over the past centuries have led to increased greenhouse gas emissions and the present rate of climate change and yet it is the countries of the 'global south' that suffer many of the major consequences and are least equipped to deal with them. Small Island States and some highly populated costal regions are in danger of sinking below a rising sea level. As a result many people will become environmental refugees. International conferences and agreements so easily fracture along developed/less developed divide and provide a potent source for disaffection and conflict. The development and sharing of more environmentally friendly technology is an urgent imperative. Ultimately efforts must be made to adopt measures to fairly distribute the emission of carbon across developed and less developed countries. The group therefore commends proposals based on equity such as 'Contraction and Convergence', promoted by the Global Commons Institute.

3.7 The Church too often retreats within comfort zones of familiar debates and mild protests, or confines its engagement to the most obvious 'headline hitting' issues. And these are precisely the times when we should be most wary. Because sin and evil are not yet finally defeated, the Christian Church is bound to be a body of protest. Complacency should worry and disturb us, though we probably cannot shake ourselves awake. Only the witness of Scripture, the peace and social justice of Christ himself, enable us to see the evil of war and violence for what it truly is. Here we learn of God's will that 'nation shall not lift up sword against nation, neither shall they learn war any more' (Isaiah 2:4b), that he will judge between the nations and arbitrate for oppressed peoples (Isaiah 2:4a; 3:13-5). Here we learn that God's anger will be kindled against nations that make iniquitous decrees, rob the people of their rights, acquire wealth at the expense of the poor, or sit by complacently while some go hungry (Isaiah 32:9-10).

3.8   Hence the importance, in our account of strategies for peace, of looking at and really seeing what is going on in the world. (Roman Catholic social teaching sometimes recommends the so-called See-Judge-Act approach in which looking and seeing is followed by judgement and action, followed by further See-Judge-Act cycles.[8]) 'Seeing', involves looking around us at the grim realities of widespread killing, the destructiveness of modern warfare, the moral implications of becoming accustomed to violence and the potential exercise of power associated with nuclear weapons, and such like.[9] We need to become more informed about international relations, to learn who is affected by warfare and how, why conflicts arose, and what our concerns are about political handling of attempts at resolution. This requires not only an inquiring and questioning attitude but also information systems that expose sins of omission and commission. We need statisticians, investigative journalists, photographers, artists, civil servants working in international development, non-governmental organisation staff, advocates for asylum seekers and refugees to help us find ways of looking that invite contemplation of, and questions about, what is due to all human beings and to God.

[8] The Roman Catholic Bishops' Conference of England and Wales, *The Common Good* (Manchester, Gabriel Publications)
[9] Members of the Working Group recommend Jim Garrison, *From Hiroshima to Harrisburg* (London: SCM, 1980) and *The Darkness of God* (London: SCM, 1982) as informed accounts of the destructiveness of modern warfare and the kind of expression of enmity asserted by nuclear weapons.

3.9 Careful discernment and nurture of vocation, so that every member of the body of Christ is encouraged to think about the career path or voluntary work to which they are called, is surely part of the Church's strategy for peacemaking – albeit not immediate in effect. The Spirit of God grants varying intensities of participation in the different aspects of peacemaking. Church members have different gifts and therefore different vocations. Relatively few church members are called to ordination and the ministry of word and sacrament. Many more are called to other vocations and part of the Church's responsibility to nurture is, we suggest, to help its members – whether retired, middle-aged or young – to discern the calling of God's Spirit into the world to find Christ there.

3.10 The more pressing question is how to move, today, from informed looking to wise judgement. Illusions of peace are all around us. We watch the news from all over the world, learn about military build-ups, the upgrading of nuclear weapons, neglected obligations under international treaties, weakened structures of accountability, the unwillingness of those 'in power' to allow others a seat at the table. The defence industries of powerful nations have obvious interests and great lobbying influence to bring to bear on governments, for economic, employment and research-related reasons.[10] How is the vision of God's peace to inform our speaking and acting? Governments also have a duty to protect their citizens: under international law, the first responsibility of the government of a sovereign state is to protect. In deciding what resources are needed to do this, governments have to predict the defence needs of the country many years ahead and against possibly unknown antagonists. At the global level, the negotiation of treaties (e.g., the quinquennial review of the Nuclear Non-Proliferation Treaty) are often fraught with tensions – especially when the US fears that its dominance is threatened by new power bases, and countries with emerging technological and economic capacities want a role in writing the rules. At the time of writing, decisions about the future of Trident are being made, and we contend below that a Christian vision of God's peace should lead members of the churches to argue against its replacement.

---

[10] Paul Rogers, *Losing Control: Global Security in the Twenty-First Century* (London: Pluto Press, 2000), examines some of the dangers and pressures in the development of armaments, including the oft-evidenced desire of governments to prove their weaponry capability. See esp. p.8.

3.11 'Protecting citizens' has, until recently, always been seen in terms of protecting people from hostile enemies outside or within the country and the 'protection' has come in the form of police and military provision as well as the brokering of treaties and the development of 'deterrents'. In the modern context a government's duty to protect its citizens must extend to responsibility for planning with other nations the mitigation of environmental problems. It demands a much greater concern over the use, disposal and recycling of the world's fresh water supplies. It also requires attention to be given to an increased likelihood of food shortages due to disruption to agricultural production. The recent Pentagon report 'An Abrupt Climate Change Scenario and its Implications for the United States National Security' discusses food shortages due to disruption and decline in agricultural production, decreased availability of water in some areas as a result of changed patterns of precipitation, more frequent extreme weather events and disrupted access to energy supplies as a result of storms.[11]

3.12 Christian political judgement can be naïve – and not in the Christ-like, child-like sense. There have also been many times when prophetic judgement has been deficient or absent. Too often, we react too late, jump on the nearest bandwagon, or satisfy ourselves with less than fully-informed comment. There are, of course, examples of church leaders lifting the eyes of the nation to the spiritual landscape within which we all operate, and even of church reports and programmes that have given insights into possibilities for change. Too often, the Church and its members have influence but do not know how to use it. All the more reason, therefore, for churches such as the United Reformed Church and the Methodist Church, to consider carefully what kind of judgement and action might be required of its members today.

---

[11] P. Schwartz and D. Randall, in *An Abrupt Climate Change Scenario and its Implications for United States National Security (Global Business Network, www.gbn.com, 2003)*

4

NON-VIOLENT STRATEGIES
FOR DEALING WITH CONFLICT

a. Rationale and inspiration

4.1 For the Church to affirm its faith in a God of peace means that wherever possible it must seek non-violent means of dealing with conflict situations. This is a broad claim and there is no shortage of possible meanings. Violence finds many manifestations – in the home and school playground, amongst gangs in our cities, words that brutalise colleagues in workplaces, and in familiar means of entertainment; the level of realism to which we are accustomed in films, video games, and such like, is graphic and detailed. It is potentially desensitising to the horror of violence and, more worrying, conducive to the illusion that violence, once started, is controllable. In real life, as opposed to technologically generated scenarios, violence has an uncontrollable and unpredictable quality with consequences that often exceed those anticipated. Our responsibility as Christian people is, we believe, always to seek non-violent solutions to problems wherever possible. Discussion is short-circuited if we concentrate too much around polarised 'pacifist' versus 'non-pacifist' positions; the challenge to find non-violence solutions to conflicts is not confined to politicians, police and military commanders, but faces us all.

4.2 Regrettably, discussions about international conflict too often polarise around pacifist / non-pacifist positions. Some 'absolute pacifists' abjure the use of force in any circumstances. Secularist versions of this position might argue on the basis of rationally held duties or ideals, or consequentialist assessments of how to minimise suffering. Christian versions include Menno Simons's sixteenth century repudiation of war because 'the truly baptised disciples of Christ know of no weapons other than patience, hope, non-resistance and God's Word.'[12] Others would regard themselves as conditional pacifists, that is, wanting to resist violence but not ruling out entirely the use of appropriate force as a last resort by a police force or a military force in a situations of gross injustice (some would use the term 'pacifistic' for this position). Whatever the terminology used, however, the priority is making the non-violent resolution of conflict an imperative that characterises our ecclesial, domestic, community, professional and political affairs. Christians know from the cost of Christ's peacemaking that this vocation will sometimes be a costly one.

---

[12] J. Horsh, *Menno Simons*, 31.

4.3   Mahatma Gandhi is an inspiration for all those who seek non-violent means of resolving conflicts. Gandhi was a Hindu who was eclectic in his religious thinking and open to ideas from Christianity, Islam and Buddhism. His admiration for the Sermon on the Mount is well known, and he said, upon first reading it, that 'it went straight to my heart'.[13] Gandhi coined the term *Satyagraha*, the 'force of truth', to signify the need to engage in struggle, albeit non-violently, for the sake of truth. He returned from South Africa in 1915, and burst suddenly into Indian politics in 1919, when he won support for a 'third way' between revolutionary nationalism and the Constitutionalists. He had some failures and many successes in the 1920s and 1930s, the latter occurring when the situation allowed for massive public protests in ways that embarrassed or wrong-footed the government and attracted widespread publicity beyond India – such as the Salt Tax March in 1930. For much of his life, he remained ambivalent about what in the West is commonly known as pacifism, yet he continues to influence Christian activists and visionaries who find resonance in his work with Jesus' teaching about selfless love.[14]

4.4   One of the best-known adaptations of Gandhian non-violence was made by Martin Luther King Jr. In the civil rights movement of the 1950s and 1960s, Gandhian non-violence became a weapon of the weak against the strong albeit culturally transformed and underpinned by a Christian theology that owed much to the social gospel movement and Reinhold Niebuhr. King joined the Gandhian techniques of Satyagraha with the Christian concept of *agape* to provide a remarkably effective means of resisting and overturning the oppression of black people in the American south. With great skill, aided by superb rhetoric, King used  non-violent protest to attract publicity outside the confines of the American South and thereby appeal to a wider audience in the hope of shifting public opinion.

---

[13] M. K. Gandhi, 'My Experiments With Truth', in *The Selected Works of Mahatma Gandhi* (Navajivan Trust: Ahmedabad, 1968), 101.

[14] 'I do believe that,' he wrote 'where there is only a choice between cowardice and violence, I would advise violence. ... Would rather have India resort to arms in order to defend her honour than that she would, in a cowardly manner, become or remain a helpless witness to her own dishonour.' M. K. Gandhi, 'Young India', 11 August 1920, in *The Complete Works of Mahatma Gandhi* Vol. XVIII (Publications Division, Government of India), 132.

4.5   More recent examples of relatively peaceful transitions of power are found in Poland, in the 1980s and 1990s when the Workers' Defence Committee and, later, Solidarity, formed a series of educational, artistic and legal networks that complemented State provision (e.g., a 'flying university' and independent underground bars/pubs) rather than confront State power head-on. These networks all contributed to radical changes in the governance of the country. The fall of the Berlin Wall is another example of non-violent popular action that, at a given time and in particular circumstances, challenged the power of an autocratic regime.[15] Yet more recently, we have seen the ability of large numbers of people to overturn by peaceful means the power of established governments in the Ukraine, and elsewhere. As the political philosopher Hannah Arendt has written: 'Popular revolt against materially strong rulers … may engender an almost irresistible power, even if it foregoes the use of violence in the face of materially vastly superior forces.'[16] In addition, many individuals and small groups around the world have kept alive a spirit of 'alternative', non-violent ways of responding to overwhelming power. Well known examples include Aung San Suu Kyi in Burma, Thich Nhat Hanh in Vietnam, the Dalai Lama, Rabbi Jeremy Milgrom – founder of Rabbis for Human Rights, and many more. None of these figures provide all the resources and ideas that we need today, but they encourage us to be bold in denouncing the fatalism that says that violence is inevitable. The working group encourages the recounting of, and contemplation of, their stories in order to generate discussion and ideas that might better enable our own non-violent living and analysis of the causes of conflicts around the globe.

[15] See Jonathan Schell, *The Unconquerable World* (London: Allen Lane, 2003).
[16] Hannah Arendt, *The Human Condition* (Chicago: University of Chicago Press, 1958), p.200.

4.6 The Bible also offers resources for non-violence action. Walter Wink interprets the Sermon on the Mount as Jesus' way of creative, loving, non-violent resistance. Concerning Matthew 5:39, 'Do not resist evil...', he points out that antistênai (to resist) is a military term implying violent resistance. The logic of the text, he says, is that disciples should not be supine or complicit in their oppression nor react violently to it. Rather, they should find a third way' 'a way that is neither submission nor assault, neither fight nor flight ... Strip naked and parade out of court, a burlesque of legality. ... Walk a second mile, surprising the occupying troops, and putting them in the wrong (they were only entitled to request assistance for one mile) ... break the cycle of humiliation with humour and even ridicule.'[17] According to Wink's interpretation, the text's central argument is that disciples of Jesus should seize the moral initiative in finding a creative alternative to violence and that, in so doing, they will assert the dignity of their own humanity. Jesus' teaching, he says, is not a call to passive acceptance of injustice and oppression but imaginative and brave, albeit non-violent, action for change. It might appear surprising in the light of this to find that Wink believes that the criteria of the just war tradition, both *jus ad bellum* and *jus in bello* 'are indispensable in the struggle to mitigate the myth of redemptive violence'.[18] Arguably, however, this underlines the need to move from entrenched positions (pacifist, pacificist, just war) to more broadly-based consensus about benefits of learning together about non-violent approaches to conflict resolution from the broad spectrum of Christian, other faith and secular reflection and practice.

---

[17] Walter Wink, *Engaging the Powers: Discernment and Resistance in a World of Domination* (Minneapolis: Fortress Press, 1992), 186-7.
[18] Wink, *Engaging the Powers,* 215.

b.   Training and strategy

4.7   If non-violence strategies are to be effective in resolving conflict, the first requirement is that they are adequately resourced. The UK contributes to peace-keeping and peace enforcement through the UN, the Department for International Development and the Foreign and Commonwealth Office. The Langley Report argues that while 6 per cent of the Ministry of Defence budget is spent on conflict prevention there needs to be a rethinking of strategy to address conflict: 'Since the end of the Cold War, conflicts globally have changed in many ways and it is clear that long-lasting security depends upon economic prosperity, co-operation and the addressing of global issues such as climate change, clean water, secure food supply and social justice.'[19]

4.8   Conflict transformation needs to take place in a preventative as well as a curative context. Avoidance of conflict by education and training is preferable to post conflict re-education programmes. It is significant that following the genocide in Rwanda it was possible to attract grants to hold conflict transformation courses, but it is much more difficult to gain funding for projects to prevent violent conflict before it begins. The techniques and material used to train people on the ground are equally applicable to pre-conflict situations where the signs of potential violent conflict are evident. Aspects covered include causes of conflict, religious teaching on justice and peace, case studies on conflict situations, and examples of effective non-violent responses to injustice and oppression. The place of mediation is essential in conflicts at every level, personal, communal, national and international, and describing the qualities and skills of a mediator and ground rules for mediation are important aspects of training. One key aspect of this mediation is facilitating 'truth-telling': enabling conflicting parties to move beyond victimhood to empathise with the suffering of those they oppose, and acknowledge the reality of their position. A variety of conflicts need to be examined so that an assessment can be made of potentially destructive conflicts and how they can be redirected to have a constructive outcome.

[19] **Chris Langley,** *Soldiers of the Laboratory Military Involvement in Science and Technology - and Some Alternatives,* Stuart Parkinson & Philip Webber, eds. (Folkestone: Scientists for Global Responsibility, 2005), 27.

4.9 Conflict transformation must also be considered in the context of resource competition. As previously discussed, a far greater level of international agreement is also now urgently needed to deal with rising sea levels and other problems associated with climate change. This is a fraught discussion in multinational gatherings often resulting in a stand-off between the developed nations and the less developed ones. Only an equitable scheme built around universal rights can hope to garner widespread support.

4.10 This limited work undertaken by government in the area of conflict prevention and peace building is supplemented by a wide range of projects by NGOs and religious groups. Resources with details of these projects are provided in the Appendix, but we offer three examples here. The Centre for Peace, Non-Violence and Human Rights, based in Osijek, Croatia, which has set up a number of projects. The Listening Project, for example, aims to build trust and mutual respect by encouraging people to express their feelings, to release their concerns, angers and fears and to enable people to articulate problems in communities. This has helped to build bridges between Serbs and Croats. A second example project is the Peace Building, Healing and Reconciliation Programme based in Nairobi, Kenya and in Kigali, Rwanda. The project seeks to train the trainers in a series of courses that use the techniques described earlier to build bridges in the polarised situation in Rwanda and Burundi and the surrounding countries in the Great Lakes area. Finally, the Methodist and URC churches support the Ecumenical Accompaniment Programme in Palestine and Israel. The mission of the EAPPI is to accompany Palestinians and Israelis in their nonviolent actions and engage in concerted advocacy efforts to end the occupation.

This morning, I met one of our neighbours when the vegetable cart stopped in the street outside. A man came past selling sweet pancakes, and she said: 'These are for when we break the fast, in the evening. Come to my house at eight, after we have broken the fast, and taste.'…

They welcomed the two men in our group, while I was ushered (pausing so that I could take off my shoes) into the living room of the house, where the women, girls and younger children were gathered….

We talked about the Ramadan pattern of prayer, and about fasting. A very beautiful young woman, looking like a nun in her hijab, talked about the restraint of Ramadan – the things from which people are to refrain. But she emphasized what is positive: the way the spirit is freed and focused (though she didn't use that word) by both fasting and prayer. She said: 'This is what God wants us to do. We do it for God. But it is good for us, too.' Out in the courtyard, I learned afterwards, the conversation among the men had also run deep: moving between the political and the personal with honesty and mutual trust. We never tasted the pancakes (perhaps the children ate them all!). What we did taste, that evening with our neighbours, was the kind of community that happens when people of goodwill take time to be human together.

(Jan Sutch Pickard, 'Come and Taste – Ramadan in Jayyous', EAPPI Report, 19 October 2005)

5

ON THE USE OF FORCE

5.1 Our approach so far has been to consider distinctly theological grounds for peacemaking, whilst taking into account the variety of Christian and other witness. Our 'baseline' assumption is that God's will for humankind is peace. His ultimate authority and peace are the original truth of the world's being and goal of our history (Isaiah 42:1–12; Romans 15:33, 16:20).[20] Also, peacemaking is the practical demand laid upon us by Jesus' teaching and example, and peace is one of the graces of character wrought by the Holy Spirit in the Church (Galatians 5:22–23). The difficult question now is whether – and, if so, when – the use of force should be tolerated. As a noted Methodist theologian of the twentieth century asked, can there ever be 'a positive use of force'?[21]

5.2 In addressing this question we need to be acutely aware of the reality of war, rather than the many myths that surround it. The Working Group therefore sought to attend to the voices of those who have fought in warfare, and those who have been victims of it. We were particularly grateful for the contribution of a military chaplain to the group's reflections, and we have included insights from a chaplain's point of view in Appendix 1. One perspective of those who serve in the armed forces is summarized in the following quotation:

Every member of the Armed Forces must be prepared to fight and die for whatever legitimate cause the UK is pursuing through military endeavour. … War is a most bloody and destructive business. … For those who have not experienced it, it will be difficult to imagine just how demanding and frightening a process war is.[22]

---

[20] For a more extended theological discussion of this point, see Oliver O'Donovan, *The Just War Revisited* (Cambridge: Cambridge University Press, 2003), p.2.

[21] Paul Ramsey, 'The Uses of Power' in *Journal of Religious Ethics* 19.2 (1991): 1-30.

[22] JWP 0-01 British Defence Doctrine.

This is the story of Harry Patch, who fought in the First World War as a Private in the Duke of Cornwall's Light Infantry:

On my 19th birthday in 1917, we were in the trenches at Passchendaele. We didn't go into action, but I saw it all happen. Haig put a three-day barrage on the Germans, and thought, "Well, there can't be much left of them." I think it was the Yorkshires and Lancashires that went over. I watched them as they came out of their dugouts and the German machine guns just mowed them down. I doubt whether any of them reached the front line.

A couple of weeks after that, we moved to Pilckem Ridge. I can still see the bewilderment and fear on the men's faces as we went over the top. We crawled, because if you stood up you'd be killed.

All over the battlefield the wounded were lying there, English and German, all crying for help. But we weren't like the Good Samaritan in the Bible, we were the robbers who passed by and left them. You couldn't stop to help them. I came across a Cornishman who was ripped from shoulder to waist with shrapnel, his stomach on the ground beside him. A bullet wound is clean - shrapnel tears you all to pieces. As I got to him he said, "Shoot me." Before I could draw my revolver, he died. I was with him for the last 60 seconds of his life. He gasped one word - "Mother". That one word has run through my brain for 88 years. I will never forget it. I think it is the most sacred word in the English language. It wasn't a cry of distress or pain - it was one of surprise and joy. I learned later that his mother was already dead, so he felt he was going to join her. [23]

[23] Cited in Max Arthur, *'Lest We Forget'*, The Guardian, 1st November, 2005.

The following story illustrates the impact of wars on those who are innocently caught up in them:

Emma Williams is a British doctor who is married to a UN negotiator; she was due to give birth to a baby around Christmas and had decided that she would like the birth to take place in the Arab Holy Family Hospital in Bethlehem. In October 2001 Israeli tanks and troops occupied Bethlehem and twenty people were killed in their attacks. The maternity hospital was fired at by a tank. Emma nevertheless kept to her intention and a few days before Christmas her child was born in Bethlehem. As Emma points out, others were not so fortunate. On 22 October a neonate died because his mother, Rawida, was denied passage as she tried to reach the hospital. The party took a 90 minute detour over rocky ground, during which time the baby was born and died. 3 days earlier Rihab Nufal was travelling from her home near Bethlehem to give birth at the hospital but was stopped by Israeli soldiers. The mother and her unborn child died whilst detained at the checkpoint.[24]

[24] Source: *The Independent*. 24 December 2001. Article by Emma Williams

From the other side of the conflict, comes this extract from a story told by a Jewish woman whose daughter was killed in a suicide bombing:

My little girl was killed because she was born Israeli, by a young man who felt hopeless to the point of murder and suicide just because he was born a Palestinian. After her death a reporter asked me how I can accept condolences from the other side. I said to her very spontaneously that I do not accept condolences from the other side. And when the mayor of Jerusalem came to offer condolences, I went to my room because I didn't want to speak to him or shake his hand. Because for me, the other side is not the Palestinians, and I believe that dividing the population into two enemy sides, Palestinians and Israelis, is a wrong and murderous division. For me the whole population of the area, and of the world has always been divided into two other distinct groups: peace lovers and war lovers.[25]

Whatever position Christians take on the legitimacy of warfare as a last resort, they must do so in knowledge of what war is like for those who are required to fight, and those who are attacked.

[25] Provided by the minister of St.Andrew's Church (Church of Scotland) in Jerusalem, 2001

5.3   The question of whether there can be a positive use of force is not categorically different from that addressed above about how to be peacemakers in our time. Both concern how to honour God and prepare for the coming of his kingdom. Both arise in a world not yet redeemed and not yet subject fully to the authority of Christ. So far, we have examined the claim that God's will is for peace and also the implication that war, violence and coercion will always be alien to God's reign. All human exercise of violence and coercive force is ontologically abnormal in the sense that it does not characterise the being of the world as God created it and wants it to be; it falls short of his purposes for it. Yet, sin and corruption are so much part of our existence, and have so many expressions, that we must reckon with their effects. We are all both victims and servants of sinful desires. We all know that the effects of the fall are such that war, violence and coercion are commonplace. In the next sections, our question is whether the threat or use of force could ever be tolerated and/or undertaken by servants of the Prince of Peace. Might violations of God's law ever be so great as to warrant the use of military force against those guilty of sins against it? Is human discernment reliable enough to make this kind of judgement? Our discussion in this section does not examine fully the ethical distinction in the application of military versus non-military forms of coercion. We identify some general principles on the use of force that might have salience for the use of economic or other kinds of sanctions, but discussion of how and when it would be appropriate to use these measures needs to be a part of a wider discussion than there is space for here.

5.4   Earthly governance has a role to play in divine providence (Matthew 22:21; Romans 13:4; Acts 25:10). The temporal authority of earthly governance is coercive, rather than persuasive, and concerns earthly rather spiritual goods. Nonetheless, it is an authority under the proviso of the grace of God. The functions of law, impartial judgement, the promotion of education and culture, general maintenance of order within which the Church can function, and more besides, are important services that earthly governance performs before God (whether or not his name is acknowledged). How, then, does the role of earthly governance within divine providence bear upon our question?

5.5   Consider two scenarios. First, the rise of Hitler to power in the 1930s and the widespread failure of the churches to oppose him – because, in part, of theologies that saw a strong state as God's remedy for sin. Hitler and his troops were welcomed and even hailed by some as an instrument of God.[26] Second, the genocide in Rwanda in 1994 which, it is argued, could have been prevented with only 5000 United Nations troops.[27] The better way in Rwanda, of course, would have been to 'see it coming' and take preventative economic, social and political measures. Even so, many of these horrific tribal killings could probably have been prevented by a stronger, international military presence exercising a creative role of restraining force.

[26] Ref. from Schölder, *The Churches and the Third Reich*.
[27] This was argued in 'Rwanda Remembered', *The Economist* March 25, 2004.

5.6 These two, rather extreme, scenarios illustrate the ambivalence that besets all human exercise of earthly governance. In one, the state took on demonic characteristics, like 'rulers of the darkness of this world' (Ephesians 6:12) or the 'beast out of the abyss' (Revelation 13:19) who blasphemed God in attempting to conquer the whole world. In the other, our pain is caused not only by the actual suffering of the people but also by the thought that stronger and more just earthly governance could, and should, have prevented this. It is in this tension that we ask whether – and, if so, when – the use of force should be tolerated. Who has the authority to make war? How does, or should, weapons proliferation and the increasing firepower available to individual and collective fighters affect decision-making? How does the Church both support earthly governors in their service of justice whilst calling for repentance before God for any, and every, act of violence?

a.   The authority to wage war

5.7 The question of authority is complex and contestable. According to what moral or legal framework is authority established, in whose eyes, over which domains, and under what conditions? The 2003 invasion of Iraq brought such questions to the fore as the world debated whether the United Nations Organisation and its Security Council was the only appropriate body to authorise war and, if so, why. Our particular question is how a Christian understanding of authority is shaped by confession of the authority of God who will establish justice throughout the earth (Isaiah 42:4; Revelation 18:10), the task being to draw out the conclusions implied in this confession for peacemaking in our context of the 'war on terror', military aggression, nuclear proliferation, and such like. In Christian moral reasoning the question of authority, and/or the right, to pursue war is subject always to the pacific authority of God. Our particular question concerns how a theological account of the authority to pursue war, or to refrain from it, proceeds from and through an account of divine authority.

5.8   This means that discussion about the authority to pursue war cannot be reduced to assertions of a nation's self defence. A decision to pursue war can only be authoritative if, like acts of judgement performed by the judiciary, the person or body making the judgement has the public standing to determine whether wrongs have been committed and, if so, how restitution and reconciliation might be effected.[28] The nature of authority in this context is that of judicial arbitration exercised on grounds that can be defended publicly – preferably that of a third party. The attacked may take to themselves the judicial role only when there is no competent third party. Armed conflict can be a possibility only when other modes of judicial authority have been exhausted or are reduced to incompetence.

5.9   Difficulties with this kind of approach arise from the sheer complexity and diversity of international relations. Traditional just war thinking maintained that the power to declare and counsel war should be 'in the hands of those who hold the supreme authority' because they have the duty to 'rescue the poor: and deliver the needy out of the hand of the sinner'.[29] The authority of a prince, says Aquinas, is necessary for a war to be deemed not sinful – along with a just cause and a right intention. In the absence of a higher or formal judicial authority, he took this authority to himself. A just war is 'one that avenges wrongs, when a nation or state has to be punished, for refusing to make amends for the wrongs inflicted by its subjects, or to restore what it has seized unjustly' (Aquinas, S.T. 2a2ae 40, c).[30] In our own time, a whole range of debates surround the question of whether the Security Council of the United Nations is the right authority for such decisions and, if so, how it should be constituted.

---

[28] Arguments to this effect have been developed recently by Oliver O'Donovan, *Just War Revisited* (Cambridge: CUP, 2003), pp.22-26.

[29] Aquinas, *Summa Theologiae*, trans. Fathers of the English Dominican Province, 1920, 2a2ae 40, art. 1, c.

[30] For a fuller treatment of traditional just war thinking, see Paul Ramsey, *The Just War: Force and Political Responsibility* (Savage, Maryland: Littlefield Adams, 1983).

5.10 In the *saeculum* – that is, the time in which we have to live, believe and proclaim the good news, earthly governments provide judgement on wrongdoing and punish the offender. They are God's 'agents working for your good' (Romans 13:4) to the extent that they perform this role. This truth claim does not translate directly into any particular form of earthly governance, even the desirability of democracy across the globe. In the present day, however, the Security Council of the United Nations Organisation has unparalleled capacity to exercise judicial authority in the face of wrongs that fall outside the scope of other jurisdictions. Despite its wounds and need for reform, it is still able to arbitrate the claims of the parties to international conflicts and exercise judgement. Secular governance is provided within God's providence to preserve the world against its self-destruction. The Church is challenged in its dealings with bodies that bear this authority to speak the truth boldly.

b. The responsibility to protect

5.11 'The Responsibility to Protect' was the title of the 2001 report of the International
Commission on Intervention and State Sovereignty, developed by the Canadian Government
and a group of major foundations in response to Secretary General Kofi Annan's challenge
to the international community to endeavour to build a consensus on how to respond in
the face of massive violations of human rights and international law.[31] The report notes the
millions of people who remain at the mercy of civil wars, insurgencies, state repression and
state collapse, and argues for a rethinking of sovereignty as the responsibility to protect
citizens, informed by reflection on what is required to protect human rights and human
security. Where states fail to exercise the responsibility to protect, the report argues, there is
a right to intervene that overrides the presumptive principle of non-intervention in the
internal affairs of other states. The report draws on the Christian just war tradition in
maintaining that the primary motive for such interventions must be humanitarian (the
criterion of right intention), that all other means of addressing the issue must have been
exhausted (last resort), that the overall benefits of the intervention must outweigh its costs
(proportionality), and that the action is likely to be successful (reasonable prospect of
success).[32]

---

[31] International Commission on Intervention and State Sovereignty, The Responsibility to Protect (Ottawa: International Development Research Centre, 2001).

[32] URC sponsored report "Non-Violent Action, A Christian Appraisal", (SCM Press, London, 1972) Methodist statement "Peace and War" (Methodist Church in Britain, Conference Agenda, 1957).

5.12 The principle that the sovereignty of states is expressed in their duty to protect their citizens resonates strongly with the theological account of political authority we have surveyed above, and therefore Christians have reason to endorse this move towards greater international protections on human rights. It is crucial, however, that the emphasis remains on the responsibility of nation states and the international community to protect citizens, rather than merely the expansion of the criterion of just cause within the just war tradition. The contrast here is between a new recognition by national and international authorities of their role and responsibility in protecting citizens, and the unwelcome alternative that the responsibility to protect is considered only when military force is being considered for other reasons. In virtually all circumstances, civilians will be best protected by the avoidance of military conflict: they suffer disproportionately from the devastating destruction caused by war. In the rare circumstances where military force is necessary, it is crucial that this is carried out under international authority and under the full constraints of the just war tradition. Usually the extreme necessity of military action is reached only when earlier opportunities of more peaceable intervention have been missed.

5.13 One example of this is the situation of Sierra Leone in 2000. At one of its meetings, the Working Group heard testimony of the drug-crazed violence of the Revolutionary United Front, who hacked limbs from adults and children and gang-raped young girls. Christian and Muslim leaders were instrumental in negotiating with the rebel factions. A small British army force intervened in a military operation against the rebel stronghold to rescue captured UN peacekeepers. The success of this operation enabled the peace process to move forward and law and order to be restored. The working group saw no alternative to employing military force in this scenario, though considered it instructive that this action was only necessary after earlier British attempts to establish a United Nations peacekeeping force with stronger rules of engagement were thwarted at the United Nations Security Council.

c.   Pre-emptive attacks

5.14 The 2004 United Nations Secretary-General's High Level Panel on Threats, Challenges and Change endorses the principle of the United Nations Security Council authorizing military action against a threat that is not yet imminent, in situations where all other means have failed.[33] The panel warns that action taken unilaterally without the consent of the wider international community remains morally and politically hazardous. This position is a significant development beyond the just war tradition, which allows for a pre-emptive military action only where the threat is imminent. Hugo Grotius provides the imagery of a drawn sword or weapon snatched up that might prompt a defensive response but adds the qualification; 'danger must be immediate … Those who accept fear of any sort as justification of pre-emptive slaughter are themselves greatly deceived and deceive others'.[34]

---

[33] Panyarachun, Anand et al, *A More Secure World: Our Shared Responsibility,* (United Nations, 2004) and Kofi Annan, In Larger Freedom. Report of the UN Secretary General, 2005.

[34] Hugo Grotius, *The Rights of War and Peace,* book II, chapter 1. Trans A C Campbell (New York: M Walter Dunne, 1901), 76.

5.15 In the internal affairs of a nation state, it is the responsibility of government to address threats to human rights and human security at an early stage, rather than waiting for them to become imminent. We endorse the principle that the United Nations should act to address security threats at an early stage. However, to do so by means of war is counter to the basic just war principle of last resort: where a threat is not imminent, there is time to work on other means of addressing the threat. The just war tradition does not allow wars aimed at preventing a threat becoming imminent, for the simple reason that this would mean that many nations would have grounds to attack their neighbours most of the time. It might be argued that action by the United Nations Security Council is of a different order, and that it can be trusted to exercise its authority with restraint. In its current configuration, however, this is by no means clear. The Security Council was not created as a judicial authority but to balance interests in furtherance of collective security, and five powerful states still have the right of veto. We do not have to look far to see inconsistencies in past judgements: the proposed intervention in Kosovo was vetoed by Russia although there was evidence that ethnic cleansing had already begun; while the use of a US cruise missile to bomb a pharmaceutical factory presumed to be producing chemical agents in Khartoum in 1998 could not attract the condemnation of the Security Council in spite of almost universal criticism world-wide.

5.16 We consider it vital that the just war tradition is not modified to make it more permissive in expanding the category of pre-emption to allow wars against threats that are not imminent. This case is clear in relation to actions of individual nation states, as the change would make the just war tradition too vulnerable to being exploited in national self-interest. We also consider, however, that efforts by the United Nations Security Council to authorize military action against threats that are not imminent should also be opposed, as in its current constitution it is not sufficiently isolated from the national interests of the most powerful nations.

d. Responding to terrorism

5.17 Since 2001, one reason for military action given by the United States and the United Kingdom has been to address the risk of terrorism. At different times, leaders have claimed that the wars in Afghanistan and Iraq were necessary to combat the threat of Islamist terrorism.[35] This led to the rapid coining of the term 'War on Terror' as an umbrella justification of military action abroad, as well as the restriction of civil liberties at home. There is only one situation where a war fought against another nation in response to terrorism could possibly be considered justifiable under just war criteria: where large scale acts of terrorism have clearly been sponsored by one nation state against another. In this context, terrorism is effectively the fighting of war by unlawful means. Even in this case, warfare will usually not be justifiable in response, because there will often be other effective ways to right the injustice and address the threat. Apart from this one possible scenario, war is always an inappropriate response to terrorism. While international terrorism does not neatly fit into either the category of crime or war, responding to it as a crime is the preferable option. Wars cannot be fought against 'Terror' — indeed use of this rhetoric may well increase the terror of a nation, rather than combating it. The terminology 'War on Terror' should be resisted because it unhappily slips between the ambiguity of 'war' used as a metaphor (such as the 'war on drugs') and real wars in which real weapons kill real people. Instead of such rhetorical myth-making, serious attention needs to be given to understanding the causes of the many forms of terrorist activity. Such attention to the reality of the phenomenon of terrorism is an essential basis to any effective response.

[35] For further discussion of this topic, see Olivier Roy, *Globalised Islam* (London: Hurst & Co, 2002).

5.18 War is extremely unlikely to be an effective response to terrorism. The case of the war on Afghanistan following the terrorist attacks on the World Trade Center and the Pentagon is worth pausing over here. There was broad international support for an attempt to locate and apprehend those responsible for planning the attacks, and for the use of military means to accomplish this in the absence of apparent alternatives. However, the war failed in this aim, failed in suppressing the insurgency that arose from the overthrow of the Taliban regime, and provoked widespread anger among Muslims particularly for indiscriminate attacks on villages. The threat of international terrorism to modern nation states at the beginning of the twenty-first century is simply unlike the threats they have previously faced, and it is becoming increasingly clear in Afghanistan and elsewhere that war is not an effective way of responding to it. In such a context, it is important to develop and resource the non-violent strategies we have surveyed above, which offer alternative means of addressing and resolving the conflicts that provoke terrorism.

e.   Arms limitation

Nuclear non-proliferation

5.19   Since the atomic bombing of Hiroshima and Nagasaki by the United States in August 1945, the limitation of nuclear armaments has become a crucial element in global security. The scale of civilian death and injury was unfortunately not unique in the Second World War: the fire-bombing of Hamburg, Dresden and Tokyo each resulted in tens of thousands of deaths. The ability to deploy this kind of destructive power in a single weapon, from a single aircraft, however, signalled the potential for limitless destruction, with very little possibility of defence. After the war, the United States continued developing its nuclear arsenal, and was soon joined by the USSR and the UK in its capability to deploy nuclear weapons. In 1968, international concern about the further proliferation of nuclear weapons led to the negotiation of the Non-Proliferation Treaty signed by the US, the UK, the USSR, and 59 other states. The treaty committed the nuclear weapons states not to transfer nuclear weapons to any non-nuclear weapons state or assist them in the manufacture or acquisition of nuclear weapons. Non-nuclear weapons state parties agreed not to develop or acquire nuclear weapons. In return, the non-nuclear weapons states are promised assistance in the development of peaceful uses of nuclear technology. The nuclear weapons states also commit themselves in article 6 to 'pursue negotiations in good faith on effective measures relating to cessation of the nuclear arms race at an early date and to nuclear disarmament, and on a treaty on general and complete disarmament under strict and effective international control.'[36] China and France, the other two states known to possess nuclear weapons in 1968 did not sign the treaty at the time, but both became parties to it in 1992. Other notable non-participants were Israel, India, Pakistan and South Africa. Israel almost certainly developed its own nuclear weapons during the 1960s, but did so covertly, and has neither confirmed nor denied the existence of the programme. India tested its first nuclear weapon in 1974, and tested a further weapon in 1998 when Pakistan conducted its first test. South Africa pursued a nuclear weapons programme in the 1980s, possibly with help from Israel, but discontinued the programme in advance of the transition to majority rule and became a signatory to the treaty in 1991. In recent years, the comparative previous success in restricting the proliferation of nuclear weapons has been significantly undermined. India and Pakistan have joined Israel in possessing nuclear weapons without apparent international censure, and fears have been expressed about the nuclear ambitions of Iraq, Iran and North Korea.

---

[36] Treaty on the Non-Proliferation of Nuclear Weapons, 12th June, 1968, United Nations, New York (see http://www.iaea.org/Publications/Documents/Treaties/npt.html).

5.20 The unusual feature of the Nuclear Non-Proliferation Treaty is that it does not apply symmetrically to all state parties to the treaty. Instead, recognizing the strategic reality that the first states to develop nuclear weapons were not prepared to relinquish them, it distinguishes between the nations who first developed nuclear weapons and are permitted to keep them, and other nations who do not belong to this group and are not permitted to join it. This weapons limitation treaty is concerned not only with the kind of weapons, but with who possesses them. The asymmetry between nuclear and non-nuclear weapons states is only sustainable if the nuclear weapons states make good on their commitment to pursue efforts towards disarmament: their failure to do so is one reason for the increasing desire of other nations not to be comparatively disadvantaged. It is also crucial that a balanced approach is taken between states seeking nuclear weapons: the lack of concern about Israeli possession of nuclear weapons is problematic at a time when Arab nations are criticized for the same ambition. A crucial contribution that the UK could make to this process in the next few years would be to decide not to renew its nuclear deterrent, which is currently under review. We hope that members of the churches will stress the importance of the example the UK could set in this context, and the difficulty of objecting to the nuclear ambitions of other nations without action of this kind.

5.21 Restricting the proliferation of nuclear weapons is clearly a crucial task to which the churches should be jointly committed. Success in arms limitation is heavily dependent on trust established through peace building initiatives, such as the development of international institutions. Part of maintaining this trust in arms negotiations is the establishment of inspection regimes that can be relied on to discover treaty breaches. Proposals for non-proliferation and counter-proliferation must be critically assessed with awareness that they may be a means of maintaining the position of the strong against the weak, rather than being to the benefit of all. Only treaties formulated to bring benefit to all parties in the long term stand any chance of enduring success.

Biological and chemical weapons

5.22 In recent discussions two other categories of weapons have often been lumped together with nuclear weapons: chemical and biological weapons. Starting in 2002, the media followed the Bush Administration in making 'weapons of mass destruction' a popular referent for the three types of weapons. However, with others we consider 'weapons of mass destruction' a misleading term, as it elides the massively devastating impact of nuclear weapons with weapons that are less effective than conventional arms. It is important not to confuse the weapons types, because chemical and biological weapons do not provide a threat on anything approaching the same scale as nuclear weapons, and so do not justify the same kinds of responses. There have been successful attempts to limit the proliferation of chemical and biological weapons, including major treaties. It is necessary to remain vigilant, but fears concerning these weapons must be kept in proportion in relation to nuclear weapons on one hand, and conventional weapons, on the other.

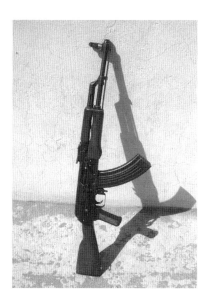

Conventional weapons

5.23 While weapons with the potential to cause death and destruction on a large scale generate the most fear among civilians, most of those who die in modern conflict are killed by small arms: revolvers, pistols, rifles, and light machine guns. The Small Arms Survey project suggests that between 60% and 90% of deaths in conflict result from the use of small arms. In 2001 it estimated that small arms killed 300,000 people annually.[37] Sales of larger conventional arms were worth around $40 billion in 2003. The major arms exporters are the US ($14 billion in 2003), the UK ($6.9 billion), Russia ($5.5 billion), France ($4.9 billion), and Israel ($2.4 billion).[38] The trade is restricted only by international arms embargoes, multilateral agreements, and the export policies of individual nation states. International arms embargoes are rare: in July 2005 there were only ten in operation.[39] There are many multilateral agreements aimed at restricting the proliferation of particular weapons types,[40] but they are limited both in their aim and effectiveness. Some states have restrictive controls on the export of weapons, but in the absence of an international treaty restricting the arms trade such as many have called for, nations are forced to balance the potential profits from selling weapons against the desire to adopt an ethical policy concerning what should be sold to whom.

[37] Graduate Institute of International Studies, *Small Arms Survey 2005*, 256–7.
[38] Source: Stockholm International Peace Research Institute Arms Transfer Project, "Financial Value of Arms Exports", URL http://www.sipri.org/contents/armstrad/at_gov_ind_data.html. The UK figure used is Ministry of Defence data for the "Value of deliveries of defence equipment and additional aerospace equipment and services" in 2003.
[39] Stockholm International Peace Research Institute, "International Arms Embargoes", URL: http://www.sipri.org/contents/armstrad/embargoes.html.
[40] For a survey, see Anthony and Bauer, 2004, *SIPRI Yearbook 2004*, 737–762.

5.24 One example of a conventional weapon that has been limited by treaty is anti-personnel land mines. The widespread deployment of these in many areas has resulted in a large number of civilian casualties long after hostilities have ended. The International Campaign to Ban Landmines estimates that in Cambodia alone there have been 35,000 amputees since conflict ended, and that worldwide there are now between 300,000 and 400,000 survivors of land mine attacks, most of whom have been permanently disabled.[41] Concern about the indiscriminate impact of these weapons, and the threat they represent to civilians long after the end of hostilities, led to a campaign to ban them, and to the 1997 Ottawa Treaty prohibiting the possession and use of anti-personnel land mines, with provision for the destruction of stockpiles. In February 2004, it had been ratified by 144 countries, but among the 42 who have not signed are China, India, Russia and the USA. Similar concerns for have been raised in relation to cluster bombs. These split into bomb-lets, and those that do not go off present a danger to civilians, and especially to children.

As Hugh Beach has observed in reflecting on the use of cluster munitions in Kosovo

The use of cluster bombs seems morally dubious. NATO officials say that about 1,100 cluster bombs were dropped, containing more than 200,000 bomblets, with a failure rate of 5%. It follows that 10,000 or more unexploded cluster bomblets remain. The post war casualty rate in Kosovo (170 up to mid-July, 1999) is reportedly comparable to Afghanistan and worse than Mozambique. Nearly half of these have been due to cluster bomblets, the remainder being due to anti-personnel mines (IHT, 20 July 1999). These figures suggest that cluster bombs deserve to join anti-personnel mines in the category of inhumane weapons.[42]

The Ottawa Treaty does not cover these weapons, yet, like landmines, they continue to represent a serious threat to civilian population, long after the end of conflict. It is therefore crucial for governments to agree to a moratorium on the use of these weapons as soon as possible.

---

[41] International Campaign to Ban Landmines, 2004, Landmine Monitor Report 2004.

[42] Hugh Beach, *Secessions, Interventions and Just War Theory: The Case of Kosovo,* Pugwash Occasional Papers I:I (February 2000).

In Basra, you do not have to go looking for cluster bomb victims. They find you.

At least Rihab did. She is a dignified woman of 28 who is wearing the extra band of black across her forehead that denotes mourning. She comes up to me and says that her brother and sister were hurt – the exact word, as translated, was "mutilated" – by cluster bombs, as was her mother, who died three weeks later. We asked if we can visit her home and the next day she takes us to Five Miles, down a crumbling alleyway to a ruined courtyard…

The battle sounds like chaos, with attack from land and air. Hamza makes the sound of a cluster bomb, as do the other family members. They point to a jagged crack in the side of the room and say that they were afraid that the house would fall down and that they decided to flee. The first group of three got as far as the street, which leads directly over the railway tracks. They were hit by shrapnel. The mother was injured in her abdomen, kidney and liver, the boy in his abdomen and bowel, and the girl on her arms and the chest. The mother died on April 16.

Ali has been in many hospitals and has had eight operations. He removes his dishdasha (an ankle-length tunic worn by Arab men) to reveal a welter of scars across his badly distended stomach. Faten, who has had two operations, pulls up the sleeve of her black abaya (a similar garment worn by women). Her arm is missing a big chunk over the elbow. They do, indeed, look mutilated. There is not an ounce of self-pity in this room, though only stoicism. I ask why. "You know," says the uncle, "we have spent three decades in a war. We are used to seeing these things".

(Ann Treneman, 'Mapped: *The lethal legacy of cluster bombs'*, The Times, 11 September 2003)

5.25 There is ongoing concern about the use of depleted uranium weapons. Enriching uranium for use in nuclear reactors and nuclear weapons creates depleted uranium as a waste product, so states with nuclear programs have significant stockpiles of the material. It is highly dense and is valuable both in armour-piercing missiles and in armour plating. However, it is both radioactive and toxic, so its use in weapons pollutes the air and the immediate environment: the spread of radio-active dust from the deployment of weapons using depleted uranium gets into the soil and the water supply and has been found to be a particular health hazard to children. For this reason the UN Human Rights Commission voted in 1996 and 1997 to ban depleted uranium weapons. However, depleted uranium weapons remain in use in many developed countries' armed forces including all the permanent members of the UN Security Council. Further investigation is necessary concerning the possible health risks to those living in areas where these weapons have been deployed. Use of these weapons must not only take into account risks to civilians, but also long-term damage to the environment.

f.   Environmental impact

5.26 All war, even war using relatively simple conventional weapons, degrades the environment. The use of chemical, biological and nuclear weapons degrades the landscape more seriously and for a far longer duration, making vast areas unusable for agriculture and residential purposes and affecting the water supplies over whole river basins. Large areas of France and Belgium were devastated by the battles of the First World War; Vietnam is still suffering from the use of Agent Orange by the USA in the 1960s. Many countries have a legacy of field testing sites for chemical and biological weapons programmes or places where they have tried to bury stocks of banned materials. There is a need for open international efforts to remediate these sites not only to stop the polluting influence from spreading but also to cut off a potential source of pathogenic materials from 'rogue states' or terrorist groups. We urgently need more research on the environmental effects of all types of munitions, international agreements to prohibit or limit their use and a robust inspection and clear up regime.

5.27 The connections between the ethics of the use of force and responsibility for the environment have not been adequately recognized. In particular, we consider they show the need for a widening of the criterion of proportionality. In weighing up the balance of benefit and harm, both when considering whether embarking on war could be justified, and when reaching a judgement about a particular action during a war, it is crucial that the environmental impact is reckoned with as part of the decision. If a war, or an attack within a war, looks likely to cause significant or long-term damage to the environment, this is in itself a reason not to proceed. The criterion of proportionality should therefore be reformulated to explicitly include the requirement to attend to environmental impact.

6

TOWARDS A CHRISTIAN VOCATION OF PEACEMAKING

6.1   For too long, Christian debates about issues of peace and war have been dominated by the question of whether force can be used in the last resort. As a result, the fundamental witness of the church to the peaceful reign of Jesus Christ has been hushed and hesitant. It is time for this to change. We call on the members and leaders of the Methodist and United Reformed churches together with other Christians to renew their commitment to be the peacemakers they are called by God to be. The Christian vocation of peacemaking is a task for the whole church, and is at once a crucial part of faithfully following Christ and a vital contribution the church makes to the earthly peace that is a basic human necessity for all people and nations.

6.2   The Christian vocation of peacemaking has four dimensions:
a. to foster just and peaceful relationships;
b. to be active in resolving conflicts;
c. to support strategies for preventing violent conflict;
d. to engage with political leaders about when and how force might be threatened or used.

a.   Fostering just and peaceful relationships

6.3   Peacemaking is not just about avoiding wars. Conflict begins on a small scale: within families, between neighbours, in churches, in schools and workplaces, among local religious and ethnic groups. They frequently arise from injustices in within such relationships, and for this reason addressing injustice is a key component of peacemaking. The lives of Christians should be distinctive in working to establish just and peaceful relationships between those among whom they live and work. This will not be a life free from conflict: conflict is an inescapable feature of human living and can often be unavoidable to bring necessary change. Peacemaking does not mean passivity, or acquiescing to injustice: it means being active in creating and maintaining right relationships. It means day by day care to deal rightly and considerately with a child, or parent, or sibling, or spouse, or friend — it may be that peacemaking in such close relationships is the most demanding of all. It means not joining factions within churches but finding common ground on which differences can be discussed, and working for understanding in differences within and between denominations. On a larger scale, peacemaking means engaging in elections and political campaigns and debates in support of policies and politicians that offer a realistic alternative to vicious cycles of hostility and fear. It means working internationally to combat economic and social threats to peace, such as poverty, infectious disease, and environmental degradation, which were highlighted in the recent U. N. Secretary-General's High Level Panel on Threats, Challenges and Change. For some Christians, being peacemakers in this context will mean working for non-governmental organizations, as civil servants or as politicians. They may undertake conflict resolution training to work in mediating between tense and divided communities at home or abroad. Through churches, political parties, and aid agencies, Christians also have a vocation to influence national and international politics, as in the Make Poverty History Campaign. On a small scale of individual relationships, through to the large scale of relationships between nations, most people are able to live in peace with one another most of the time because of the day-to-day building up of the foundation of peaceful relationships. The sustaining of such relationships is a basic part of Christian peacemaking, and through its international networks, in prayer and in action, the church is uniquely placed to assist in this task.

6.4   Fostering peaceful relationships also has an environmental dimension. Individual Christians and Churches can work to limit their ecological footprint through careful use of energy and insulation of building as well as with their use of transport. Christians together form an important constituency for the support of government action to reduce global warming. Issues of environmental concern and of global justice go hand in hand and Christians are one group, together with like-minded groups in society that can keep this fact before governments. Creating a context for peace means looking into the future, pushing political parties away from the short-term political cycle to cross party agreements that can yield a consistent and committed stance both to reduce environmental and resource causes of conflict and to mitigate those effects already apparent.

b.   To be active in resolving conflicts

6.5   There are times when the strength of relationships is not adequate for the pressures they are subjected to, and individuals or communities become locked in conflict. There is then a second task of peacemaking: that of acting to resolve conflicts. Again, we must recognize in this context that some forms of conflict are a necessary stage to a just peace; again, this task of peacemaking may be on a small or large scale; again, in different ways this is a task for the whole church. It may take the shape of overcoming hurt in order to initiate reconciliation with a close family member, or it may be represented in UN sponsored inter-governmental talks over a border dispute. It requires particular skills: patience in listening to the concerns of different parties, creativity in finding ways to enable the challenging 'truth-telling' that allows groups to acknowledge the suffering of others, wisdom in devising possible resolutions that promise benefits to each side. Beyond their role in resolving conflict in their personal and professional relationships, Christians may be called to wider involvement in this task. They may be called to volunteer as counsellors for those whose marriages are under strain. They may become specialists in arbitration of industrial conflicts. Or they may undertake conflict resolution training to work in mediating between tense and divided communities threatened by violence at home or abroad. The task of conflict transformation is dramatically under-resourced in comparison to the personnel and finance devoted to winning military conflicts, and church members and leaders, like others concerned to promote peace, should support a substantial new commitment to resourcing conflict resolution projects on an international basis by the United Nations and other international agencies.

Supporting strategies for preventing violent conflict

6.6 Alongside attempts to resolve conflicts, there may be a need to take measures to prevent the conflict expressing itself in violence, or preventing an existing violent conflict from widening or intensifying. Here the peacemaking task is that of physically separating opposing parties, and taking steps to maintain law and order. Acting to resolve situations of injustice will again be crucial in this task. This is what a teacher may do in dealing with a brawl at school; it is what police forces are tasked with when controlling crowds at football matches; it has been the role of UN authorized peacekeeping troops in many places where war has threatened. In the conflict between Israel and Palestine, non-violent activists have attempted to prevent the escalation of violence by lying in front of Israeli bulldozers about to destroy Palestinian homes, and by riding Israeli buses threatened by Palestinian suicide bombs. In any form, this conflict prevention can be a costly activity, as in seeking to prevent aggression peacemakers may make themselves the target of it. Recent reminders of this are the death of the U.S. peace activist Rachel Corrie in the Gaza Strip in 2003, and the death of the U.K. peace activist Tom Hurndall in 2004 after being shot while attempting the rescue of a Palestinian child. For followers of Jesus Christ it should come as no surprise that making peace may require personal sacrifice: and for a few the vocation to peacemaking may mean putting themselves literally in the firing line. On a broader front, Christians should be supportive of prompt international action to prevent the outbreak of conflict: recent examples of lamentable inaction by the international community include Rwanda and the former Yugoslavia, where in both cases there were warnings about what was likely to take place. The deployment of troops in a peacekeeping role where conditions allow is a valuable contribution that nation states can make through the United Nations, and efforts must be made to improve the resources and decision making processes for these initiatives.

d. **Engaging with political leaders about when and how force might be threatened or used**

6.7 Even in relation to the political question of when a nation state is entitled to go to war, there is still common ground between Christians that adopt pacifist and just war perspectives:

i. Both can agree that war should never be employed 'where other means of addressing a conflict remain open. In virtually all circumstances, therefore, the word of the churches to the nation will be that the cost of war is such that nations should continue to pursue diplomatic and non-violent modes of dialogue and coercion to the utmost. In the context of the just war tradition, this is the demand to take the criteria of last resort and proportionality with utmost seriousness.

ii. When a nation has determined to go to war, both pacifist and non-pacifist Christians have a stake in seeking to hold nations accountable to the just war criteria for how wars should be fought. Christians cannot wash their hands of responsibility for a nation at war, even if the war was against their wishes. They should demand that nations conduct warfare discriminately — doing everything possible to avoid non-combatant casualties — and proportionately — ensuring that the military objective sought in an attack justifies the destruction that will be caused. They should require that nations take seriously that military action must aim at the establishment of a sustainable peace.

iii. There are times when Christians should join in asking a nation state to deploy troops in order to prevent a humanitarian catastrophe. This is clearest in the case of United Nations peacekeeping missions, but may extend to using military force to restore law and order to situations of extreme lawlessness, such as in the situation of Sierra Leone in 2000, discussed above.

iv. In relation to the issue of whether just war criteria should be revised to make it easier to justify wars fought to prevent threats, we consider that Christians taking pacifist and just war positions should together resist moves to make the just war tradition more permissive. The tradition has good reason to allow pre-emptive attacks only when the threat is immediate. To allow nations to go to war to prevent other nations threatening them, even if authorized by the current United Nations Security Council, would be to make wars more common, and international relations less secure.

v. Christians should also make common cause in supporting international attempts to limit the proliferation of arms. Nuclear weapons are the most urgent priority in this area and we consider that Church members should oppose the renewal of the UK's Trident nuclear deterrent. In the absence of imminent nuclear threat, church members should urge the UK government to make bold and immediate steps to meet its disarmament obligations in full. Without such moves, it is hard to see the justification for opposing the acquisition of nuclear weapons by non-nuclear powers. Church members should also support attempts to control the trade in conventional weapons, including small arms, which cause the majority of casualties in war. As a major arms exporter, the UK has particular responsibilities and opportunities in this regard.

Beyond this common ground, we recognize that Christians will sometimes differ amongst themselves about whether a particular war is morally legitimate. There will be times when some Christians believe that a war can be justified within the just war tradition, and others do not, either because they interpret the tradition differently, or because on pacifist grounds they believe no wars can be justified. In such circumstances, Christians will have to debate between themselves and with politicians on the basis of their best judgement. We must resist the temptation, however, to make this occasional disagreement the focus of Christian discussion of warfare. To do so is to mistake a narrow peripheral difference for the heart of Christian reflection on warfare: the need to work towards and call the nation towards a more peaceful world, in the name of the Prince of Peace.

6.8   Calling for more peaceful living in the midst of a violent world will often be seen as naive, foolish, or irresponsible. We do not accept that it is any of these things. Indeed, our claim is that a realistic appraisal of the global situation at the beginning of the twenty-first century makes clear the need for an alternative to war as a mode of resolving conflict. We do recognize, however, the influence of Christian hope on our reflections, which Paul numbered alongside faith and love in 1 Corinthians 13. The outlook for international relations often looks bleak, but members of Christ's church are not at liberty to despair, because of their faith that this is a world of which Jesus Christ is Lord, and in which his disciples are called to works of love in his name. To sustain such loving service, which includes the peacemaking we commend in this report, is possible only in the hope that the realization of peace between the nations is in God's hands. When Jesus Christ confronted the political and religious powers of his day, he chose to ride on a donkey in fulfilment of the prophecy of Zechariah that a new king would come who was 'righteous and having salvation, gentle and riding on a donkey', who would proclaim peace to the nations, and whose rule would extend 'from sea to sea, from the River to the ends of the earth' (Zechariah 9:9–10, Matthew 21:5). It is in that hope that we call on Christians as members and leaders of churches to take up the task of peacemaking in every sphere of their lives, and to call on the leaders of the nations to join them in seeking out the way of peace.

7
APPENDICES

APPENDIX 1

What is war like? A chaplain's perspective

APPENDIX 2

An account of the bombings in London, 7 July 2005

APPENDIX 3

Further reading

APPENDIX 4

Useful organizations

APPENDIX 5

United Reformed Church General Assembly Resolution

APPENDIX 1

What is war like? A chaplain's experience

For most of us, thinking about the horrors of war and weaponry remains just that –thinking. For some, it is much more demanding. In this section, we offer reflections on what war is like, written from the perspective of serving chaplains, and drawing on recent experiences.

Whatever political, sociological or anthropological language one uses to define war, words alone do little to communicate the real, abject horror of being caught up in its prosecution. Only those who have suffered its consequences, as combatants or innocent civilians, are able to bear witness to its true cost, not just in headline grabbing body counts but in the living memory of those who 'survive to tell their tale'. The real irony of such a phrase is that the survivors of war often participate in a conspiracy of silence, protecting themselves and humanity at large from the dreadfulness that is 'the cost of war'.

In all the major conflicts of modern time chaplains have accompanied armed forces into situations of conflict, not, as some would claim, to placate the 'guilt laden military monster eagerly devouring the life of others' but to be ambassadors of the Kingdom of peace and justice through 'quiet, understated witness, good counsel and prayer'. (Revd M A O'Keefe CF) '(Our role) is not to bless the terrible things that happen in war, but to be a sign of the presence of God especially in the darkest of times.' (Revd Ivan Boyle RAF) Such presence is thoroughly incarnational for even the most ardent of Christian pacifists could not deny the ministry of the churches to those who 'fight and die for whatever legitimate cause the UK is pursuing'.

Ministry in the context of war demands immense sacrifice from the chaplain, it is the greatest of privileges and a life changing experience:

On the Sunday before the conflict began, we held a service of dedication – a chance to pause and pray before we went to war. The service was short but very moving and attracted a large congregation. People had a chance to make their peace with God before facing the dangers of war. It felt a very special privilege to be able to help them do so … all in all an unforgettable experience – one I would not have missed for the world and yet would not have wished on anybody. Such is the ambivalent nature of what we do.

(Revd Jonathan Beach RAF)

To speak the things of God while others plan and execute the path of war may be seen as an irrelevance, but many chaplains, and indeed others, have testified to the importance of their prophetic role:

Another reaction to the daily "thought for the day" came in a newspaper article written by Burham Wazir, a journalist from the Guardian who accompanied our regiment for a few weeks: In contrast with the rough and tumble and understandably macho gestures of the rest of the regiment, Swinn is a quiet presence … It is during the morning meetings, however, that Swinn comes to life. When his turn comes he holds up some notes and, with shaking hands, begins what he announces as his "thought for the day". Earlier this week he read from Psalm 68. His reading was well measured and tempered with the universal fears of the days ahead. Two days ago, he said more simply "just because we have forgotten Jesus, it does not mean that he has forgotten us".

In general, I have noted a respectful hush descend upon *the table whenever Swinn speaks. Perhaps in an age where politicians prefer to openly speak of "collateral damage" and "friendly fire", the sight of an obviously nervous man, shakily delivering a simple sermon, strikes a simple and much needed profundity about the days ahead. The role of a priest might strike some as an anachronism in these modern times but I must confess to having been seduced by the simplicity of the notion. In my time here I have come to look forward to Swinn's talks. Similarly the regimental officers seem to appreciate his words …*

The biblical image of the prophet echoes to this day, in the voices heard at the anti-war demonstrations through to the battlefield. The physical and emotional cost of war is felt as deeply by the chaplain as it is the unit they are attached to. The Reverend Tudor Botwood RN recounts an experience that could be echoed by many:

I was awoken by Commander ME in the early morning with the words "there's been a helicopter crash, you had better get up to the boat bay". … The first body was brought on board, but it was not just a body it was X, someone I knew … I took the decision to make myself part of the recovery team … it helped me mourn, it gave me a sense of satisfaction to know that they (the deceased) were treated in a sensitive, and spiritually appropriate way.

The military community will often receive the 'voice of the church' as negatively critical of its very existence, which can have the effect of isolating serving personnel from the pastoral support of the churches on an institutional level. To suggest that such support is communicated through the presence of chaplains alone is surely not enough – it is beholden on the churches to find means of engaging with the decision makers in Government and the Ministries whilst also offering a pastoral voice of concern and support for those who are 'under authority'.

The military covenant makes clear that 'conflict is still the province of chaos, danger, exhaustion, fear, loneliness and privation', into such a province the chaplain speaks the words of faith 'the body and blood of our Lord Jesus Christ, which was given for thee, preserve thy body and soul unto everlasting life: take, eat and drink in remembrance that Christ died for thee, and feed on him in thy heart by faith with thanksgiving.'

APPENDIX 2

An account from the London bombings of 7 July 2005

7 July 8:50am - Our circle line train left Paddington packed with sleepy commuters. Shortly before Edgware Road there was a bang and a jolt. The carriage filled with smoke as our train rapidly came to a stop. A train passing in the other direction stopped opposite us. The lights were off on that train so we couldn't see into the carriage but screams could be heard. We eventually broke a window to get access and I and a few others with first aid training climbed through.

I had not realised at this stage that the bang we had heard was an explosion. I was suddenly surrounded by an indescribable scene of carnage, death, chaos and fear. A different world. The explosion clearly had been massive, ripping a huge hole in the floor, creating piles of debris and blasting loose clothing off those killed or injured. Seven people died in this incident. I think that 4 or 5 had probably been killed instantly by the blast. I had never encountered death at close quarters before, let alone a scene like this.

There wasn't much opportunity at the time to dwell on the scene. It took half an hour or so before the medics could get to the carriage to treat those with serious injuries meanwhile we did what little we could. In the following days, though, the events of the incident replayed through my mind like a video tape to the extent that it was difficult to think about anything else. I found it difficult to relate to the loss felt by family members of those killed. It is not easy to grieve for someone you do not know, yet the deaths of those I had seen and the trauma of those injured, affected me deeply. For many of those caught up in the 7 July incidents, dealing with the shock took days or in some cases weeks.

On reflection, I think that those present witnessed a different side to the behaviour of London commuters. As our train filled with smoke people set about reassuring others and assisting those injured. As a result calm was quickly restored. Travellers on the London Underground are notorious for their lack of interaction with each other, yet in an instant people went out of their way to meet the needs of people they had never previously encountered. It has since caused me to view disgruntled or sleepy fellow travellers on the underground through slightly different eyes.

In the week following the bombing 50 people were killed in explosions in Iraq. Israel experienced its first suicide bombing for many months and in Gaza a young woman was killed as a result of Israeli military action. The images we see on TV can't convey the personal experience of those caught up in these incidents - the shock of those who happened to be in the wrong place at the wrong time, or the grief of family members of those killed who must learn to live with their loss. Heaven forbid that we should ever become so familiar with such images that we overlook the trauma and loss of those involved.

APPENDIX 3
FURTHER READING

Ariarajah, S. Wesley, *Axis of Peace Christian faith in Times of Violence and War* Geneva: WCC, 2004.

Annan, Kofi, *In Larger Freedom: Towards development, security and huan rights for all.* www.un.org

Bailie, Gil, *Violence Unveiled: Humanity at the Crossroads.* Crossroad: New York, 1995.

Bainton, Roland H., *Christian Attitudes toward War and Peace: A Historical Survey and Critical Re-Evaluation,* Nashville, TN: Abingdon Press, 1960 .

Beach, Hugh, and David Fisher, *Just Assassination.* CCADD

Blyth, Myra and Wendy Robins, *Easter People in a Good Friday World: Witnessing Christ in the Conflict of Life,* CTBI Publications 2005.

Bruce, Steve, *Politics and Religion.* Polity Press, Cambridge, 2003.

Cadoux, John C., *The Early Christian Attitude to War,* New York: Seabury Press, 1982.

Chapman, Colin. *Whose Promised Land?* Oxford: Lion, 2002.

Chase, Kenneth and Jacobs, Alan, *Must Christianity be Violent? Reflections on History, Practice and Theology.* Brazos Press, Grand Rapids, 2003.

Christian Aid, *The Damage Done: Aid, Death and Dogma,* 2005.

Church of Norway, Vulnerability and Security *www.kirken.no/english/engelsk.cfm?artid=5850*

Ellis, Marc H. *Towards a Jewish Theology of Liberation.* London: SCM, 1987.

Elshtain, Jean Bethke, *Just War against Terror: The Burden of American Power in a Violent World,* New York: Basic Books, 2003.

Fellowship of Reconciliation. *Sowing Peace, Reaping Justice. Peacemaking in the 21st Century.* Clopton: FOR, 2004.

Francis, Diana, *Rethinking War and Peace,* Pluto Press, London, 2004

Frost, Brian. *The Politics of Peace.* London: DLT, 1991.

Garrison, Jim. *From Hiroshima to Harrisburg.* London: SCM, 1980.

Garrison, Jim. *The Darkness of God.* London: SCM, 1982.

Griffith, Lee, *The War on Terrorism and the Terror of God,* Grand Rapids, Mich.; Cambridge: W.B. Eerdmans, 2002.

Hallock, Dan. *Bloody Hell: The Price Soldiers Pay.* Farmington: Plough, 1999.

Harries, Richard (Chair), *Countering Terrorism: Power, Violence and Democracy post 9/11.* A Report by a working group of the church of England's Hosue of Bishops, House of Bishops of the Church of England 2005.

Howard, Professor Sir Michael, War against Terrorism, a talk on 30/10/01 Harris, E - 2001, *Buddhism and war: a study of cause and effect from Sri Lanka, Culture and Religion,*2 (2): 197-222.

Hunter, David G., *A Decade of Research on Early Christians and Military Service,* Religious Studies Review vol. 18, no. 2, 87–94.

Lind, Millard C. *Yahveh is a Warrior.* Scottdale: Herald Press.1980.

Long, Edward LeRoy Jr, *Facing Terrorism: Responding as Christians,* Louisville; London: Westminster John Knox, 2004.

McTiernan, Oliver, *Violence in God's Name: Religion in an Age of Conflict.* London: DLT, 2003.

Matthews, Dylan, *War Prevention Works,* Oxford Research Group 2001.

Musto, Ronald G., *The Catholic Peace Tradition,* Maryknoll, N.Y: Orbis, 1986.

O'Donovan, Oliver, *The Just War Revisited,* Cambridge, UK; New York: Cambridge University Press, 2003.

Muller-Fahrenholz , Geiko. *The Art of Forgiveness.* Geneva: WCC, 1997.

Panyarachun, Anand et al, *A More Secure World: Our Shared Responsibility,* United Nations 2004.

Parker, Russ. *Healing Wounded History.* London: DLT, 2001.

Quinlan, Michael, *'Don't give up on the Just War',* The Tablet, 19/7/03.

Ramsey, Paul, *The Just War: Force and Political Responsibility,* Savage, Maryland: Littlefield Adams, 1983.

Reed, Charles, *Just War?* London, SPCK, 2003.

Rogers, Paul. *Losing Control: Global Security in the 21st Century.* London: Pluto, 2000.

Schell, Jonathan, *The Unconquerable World,* Allen Lane, 2003.

Stassen, Glen, Ed., *Just Peacemaking: Ten Practices for Abolishing War,* Cleveland, Ohio: Pilgrim Press, 1999.

UN Responsibility to Protect

UN In Greater Freedom

Williams, Rowan, *Just War Revisited, Lecture to the Royal Institute of International Affairs*, October 2003, www.archbishopofcanterbury.org

Wink, Walter. *Engaging the Powers.* Minneapolis: Fortress, 1986.

Yoder, John H., *The Original Revolution,* Eugene, Oregon: Wipf and Stock, 1998.

Yoder, John H., *Nevertheless : A Meditation on the Varieties and Shortcomings of Religious Pacifism,* Christian Peace Shelf Series, Scottdale, Pa: Herald Press, 1971.

APPENDIX 4

Useful Organisations/Peace-building Groups

Bradford University,
Department of Peace Studies
www.brad.ac.uk/acad/peace/

Campaign Against Arms Trade
www.caat.org.uk
11 Goodwin St, London N4 3HQ
020 7281 0297
enquiries@caat.demon.co.uk

Centre for the Study of Forgiveness
and Reconciliation
a.rigby@coventry.ac.uk

Clergy Against Nuclear Arms
David Partridge, Interfaith Centre,
2 Market St, Oxford OX1 3EF
01865 202 745
dp_peace@hotmail.com

Christian Campaign for Nuclear
Disarmament
162 Holloway Rd, London N7 8DQ
020 7700 420
cnd@gn.apc.org

Community for Reconciliation,
John Johansen-Berg,
12 Ranoch Av,
Worcester WR5 3UN
01905 767 366
johnjoberg@tiscali.co.uk
www.cfrbarnesclose.co.uk

Conscience
info@conscienceonline.org.uk
www.conscienceonline.org.uk

Control Arms
www.controlarms.org

Council on Christian Approaches to
Defence and Disarmament (CCADD),
5 Cubitt's Meadow, Buxton,
Norwich, NR105EF
ccadd@lineone.net

Coventry University –
Peace & Reconciliation Studies
www.coventry.ac.uk
and Centre for the Study of
Forgiveness and Reconciliation

Ecumenical Accompaniment
Programme in Palestine & Israel,
www.eappi.org

Fellowship of Reconciliation,
St James Church, Cowley, Oxford
www.for.org.uk

Housemans Peace Diary,
diary@housemans.idps.co.uk

Initiative on Conflict Resolution &
Ethnicity, Belfast
www.incore.ulst.ac.uk

International Alert, London,
www.international-alert.org

Landmine Action,
www.landmineaction.org

Methodist Peace Fellowship,
Maurice Wright,
3 Cornwall Drive,
Shrewsbury SY3 OEP
01743 873 633
mhw@surfree.co.uk

Movement for the Abolition of War,
11 Venetia Rd, London N1 1EJ
020 8347 6162
www.abolishwar.org.uk

Network of Christian Peace
Organisations,
www.ncpo.org.uk

Pax Christi,
www.paxchristi.org.uk

Peace Direct,
www.peacedirect.org

Peace News,
www.peacenews.info

Peace Pledge Union,
enquiry@ppu.org.uk
www.ppu.org.uk

Responding to Conflict,
Birmingham,
www.respond.org

Royal Institute for International Affairs
www.riia.org

Saferworld, general@saferworld.co.uk
www.saferworld.org.uk

Scottish Centre for Nonviolence
nonviolence@callnetuk.com
www.nonviolence-scotland.org.uk

Soros Foundation
www.soros.org

UNA-UN
Decade for a Culture of Peace
www.una-uk.org
www.ministryforpeace.org.uk

United Methodist Church,
General Board of Church and Society,
www.umc-gbcs.org

United Reformed Church
Peace Fellowship,
Hazel Barkham,
The Croft, North Rd, Mere BA12 6HQ
01747 861
hazelbarkham@waitrose.com

World Conference of Religions for
Peace, 125 Salisbury Rd,
London NW6 6RG
Hopeis@btinternet.com
www.religions for peace.org.uk

World Council of Churches,
Decade to Overcome Violence
www.overcomingviolence.org

World Court Project,
geowcp@gn.apc.org
www.gn.apc.org/wcp

World Disarmament Campaign,
PO Box 28209 Edinburgh EH9 1ZR

APPENDIX 5
United Reformed Church Resolution

General Assembly mindful that in recent decades military technology has developed substantially, that definitions and terminology for various acts of warfare have been evolving, and that the politics of conflict has moved into a new, post-Cold-War era, asks its Church and Society Committee to explore and prepare a report on the ethics of warfare for the twenty-first century.

The report should take account of;

a) an understanding of terrorism, suicide bombing and state sponsored assassination

b) weapons of mass-destruction, including nuclear, chemical, biological and multi-kiloton [conventional] bombs

c) weapons which continue to cause death and suffering in a post-conflict era, e.g. land-mines, unexploded cluster-bombs, depleted uranium dust.

d) the argument that a perceived threat is justification for a pre-emptive attack, or that "regime change" is a legitimate objective for armed aggression.

e) other matters germane to the concept and practice of 'Total War'

In whatever methodology it adopts the Committee is encouraged to take account of past General Assembly resolutions and to work ecumenically and internationally.